AUTOMOBILE ENGINEERING DIPLOMA & ENGINEERING MCQ

MANOJ DOLE

Made with ♥ on the Notion Press Platform
www.notionpress.com

Contents

Foreword

Automobile Engineering Diploma & Engineering MCQis a simple Book for Automobile Diploma & Engineering Course, Revised Syllabus, It contains objective questions with underlined & bold correct answers MCQ covering all topics including all about the latest & Important about Automobile Mechanics, Applied Science Lab, Automobile Workshop Practice, Auto Electrical and Electronics, Automobile Workshop Tech, Auto Repair and Maintenance, Automotive Engine Auxiliary Systems, Automobile Chassis and Transmission, Automotive Engines, Automobile Machine Shop, Automotive Estimation and Costing, Automotive Pollution and Control, Engine and Vehicle Testing Lab, Basic Computer Skills lab English Communication, Basic Electrical and, Electronics Engineering, Hydraulics, Pneumatics and Power Plant, C Programming, CAD Practice, Machine Design and Theory of M/Cs, Computer-Aided Engineering, Graphics, Mechanical Testing Lab, Modern Vehicle Technology, Thermal engineering I, Motor Vehicle Management, Vehicle Maintenance, Organizational Management, Vehicle Maintenance Lab, Project, Industrial Visit, and Seminar, Foundry, Welding and Sheet Metal Practice, Special Vehicle and Equipment, Strength of Materials and lots more.

We add new question answers with each new version. Please email us in case of any errors/omissions. This is arguably the largest and best Book for All engineering multiple choice questions and answers.

As a student you can use it for your exam prep. This e-Book is also useful for professors to refresh material.

Preface

This book may be purchased for educational, business, or sales promotional use. Online edition is also available for this title. For more information, contact our corporate/institutional sales department: [+919921582799] or [manojdole1@gmail.com]

While every precaution has been taken in the preparation of this book, the publisher and authors assume no responsibility for errors or omissions, or for damages resulting from the use of the information contained herein.

About the Author

MANOJ DOLE is an Engineer from reputed University. He is currently working with Government Industrial Training- Institute as a lecturer from last 12 Years. His interest include- Engineering Training Material, Invention & Engineering Practical- Knowledge etc.

CHAPTER ONE

Automobile Engineering Hand Tools & Measuring Instruments Theory

Download App
Online Test Exam
ITI Books
AutoCAD CAM
JOB & Apprentice
Online Theory
Computer Course
Trading Course
CNC Course
MSCIT Course
Shopping Business
Internet Business
Web Designing
Online Services
Top Sportsmans
Indian Army
Freedom Fighters
Top Scientists
Social Reformers
Motivational Speaker
Top Richest People
Join WhatsApp Group
Join Facebook Group
Like Facebook Page
PAN / Adhar / Licence
Passport

Fire extinguisher

Calliper

Hacksaw frame

Universal surface guage

Hammer

Centre punch

Bench vice

Files

Scraper

Surface Plate

Outside Micrometer

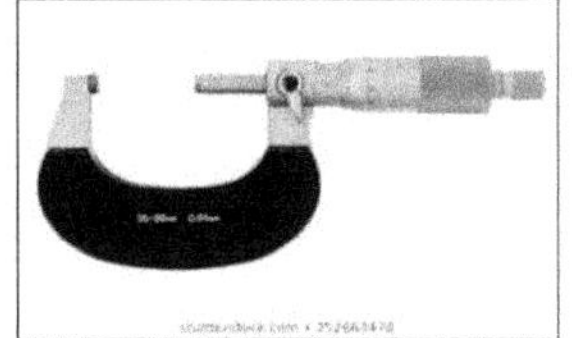

Micrometer

Depth micrometer

Vernier Calliper

Vernier bevel protractor

Drilling

Reamer

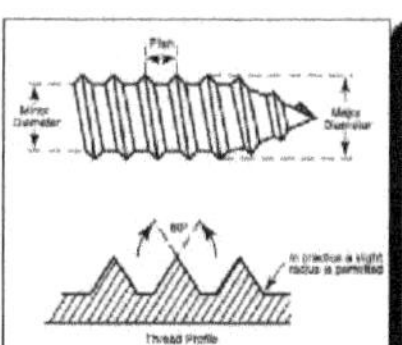

Thread

Tap Die

Grinding Wheel

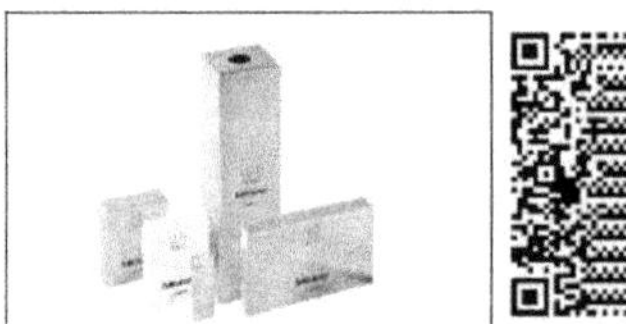

Slip gauge

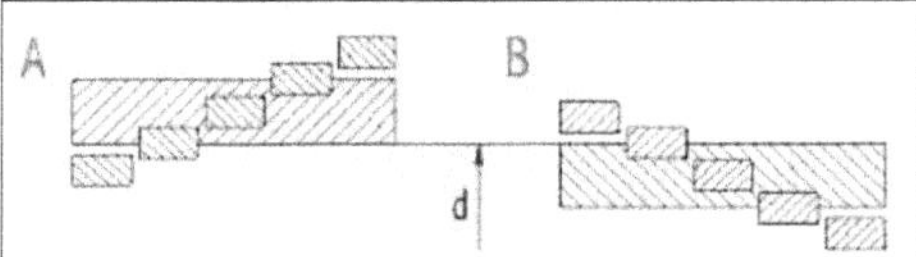

Limit fit tolerance

taper ring gauge

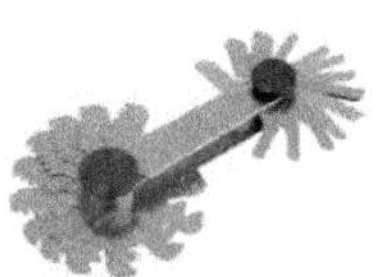

screw pitch gauge

Gear

screw pitch gauge

Tap Die

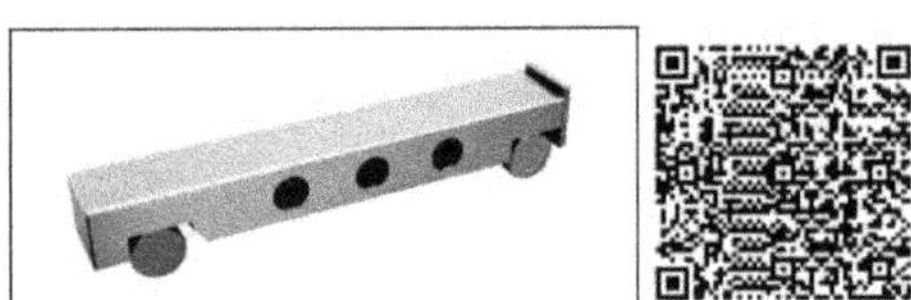

Sine bar

Slip gauge

Dial test indicator

Telescopic gauge

Feeler gauge

Centre gauge

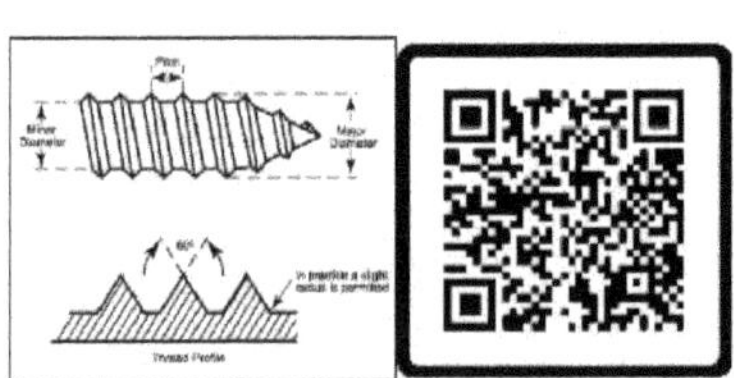

Thread

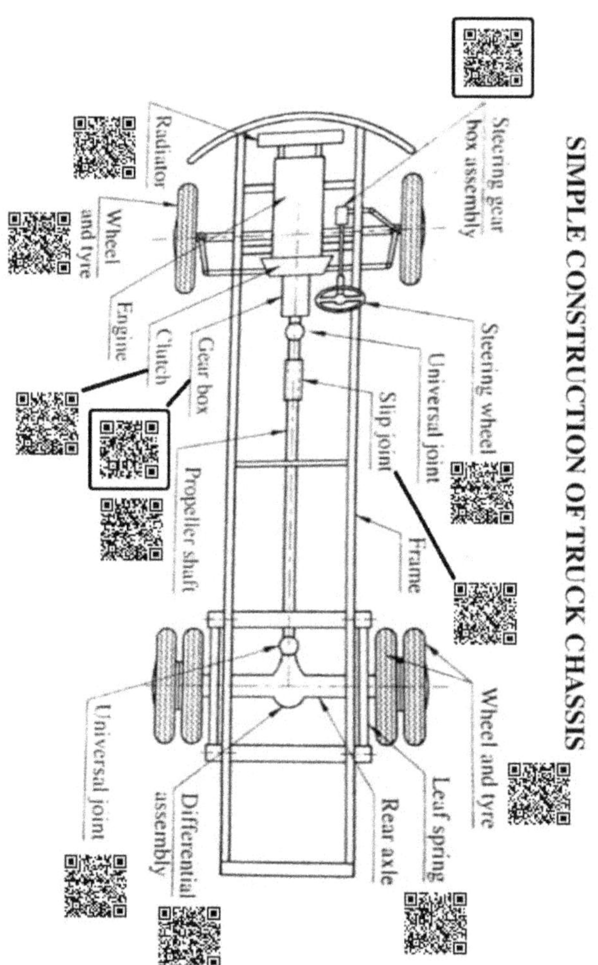
SIMPLE CONSTRUCTION OF TRUCK CHASSIS
Steering gear box assembly
Radiator
Wheel and tyre
Engine
Clutch
Gear box
Steering wheel
Universal joint
Slip joint
Frame
Propeller shaft
Wheel and tyre
Leaf spring
Rear axle
Differential assembly
Universal joint

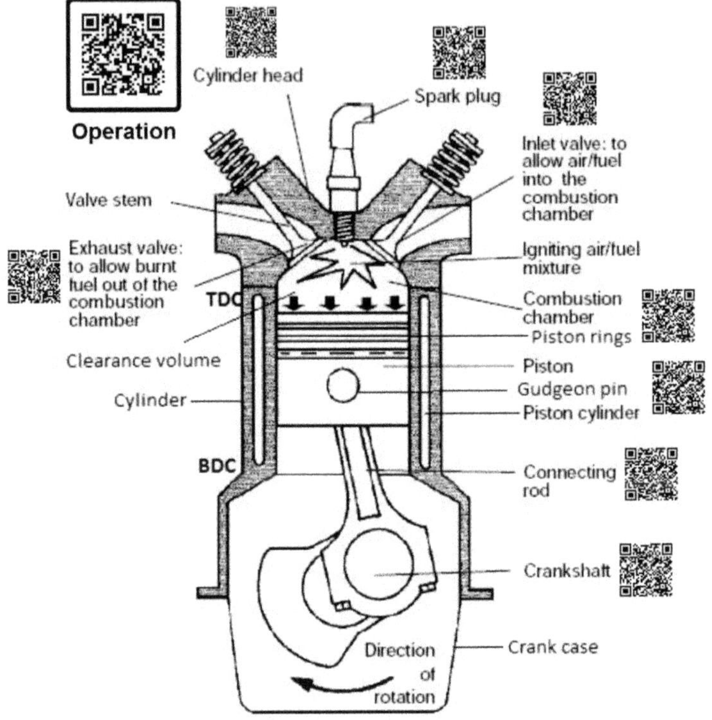

Petrol Engine Details

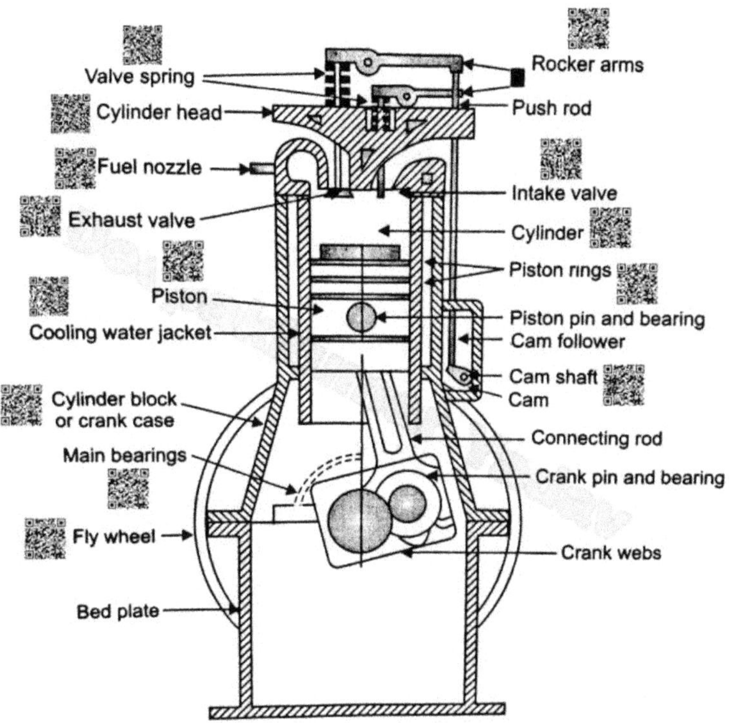

Components of Diesel Engine

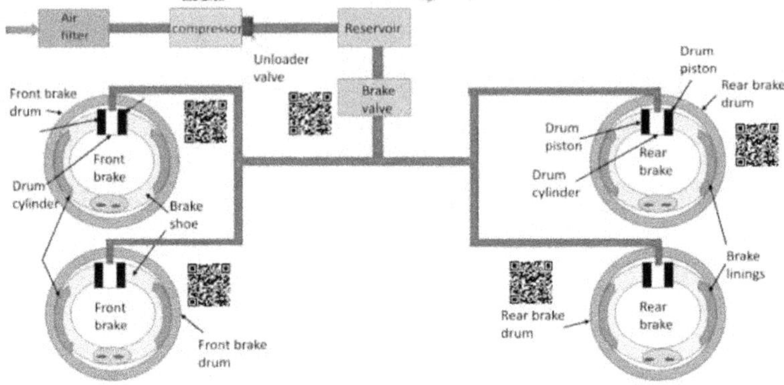
Air Braking system
Air filter
compressor
Reservoir
Unloader valve
Brake valve
Front brake drum
Front brake
Drum cylinder
Brake shoe
Front brake
Front brake drum
Drum piston
Rear brake drum
Drum piston
Rear brake
Drum cylinder
Brake linings
Rear brake drum
Rear brake

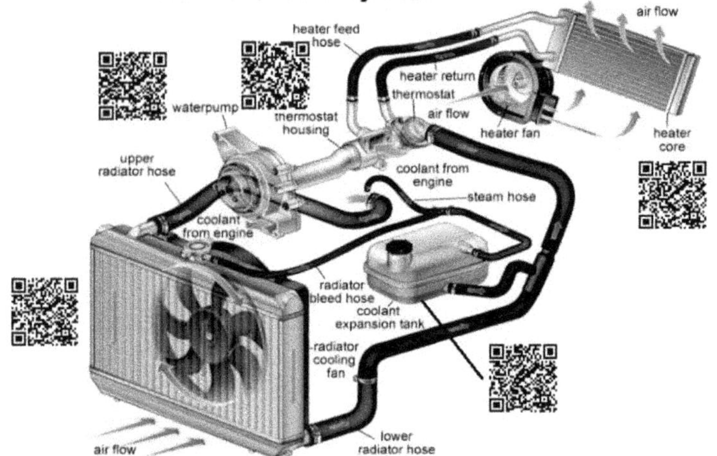
Auto Coolant System
air flow
heater feed hose
heater return
thermostat
air flow
heater fan
heater core
waterpump
thermostat housing
upper radiator hose
coolant from engine
steam hose
coolant from engine
radiator bleed hose
coolant expansion tank
radiator cooling fan
lower radiator hose
air flow

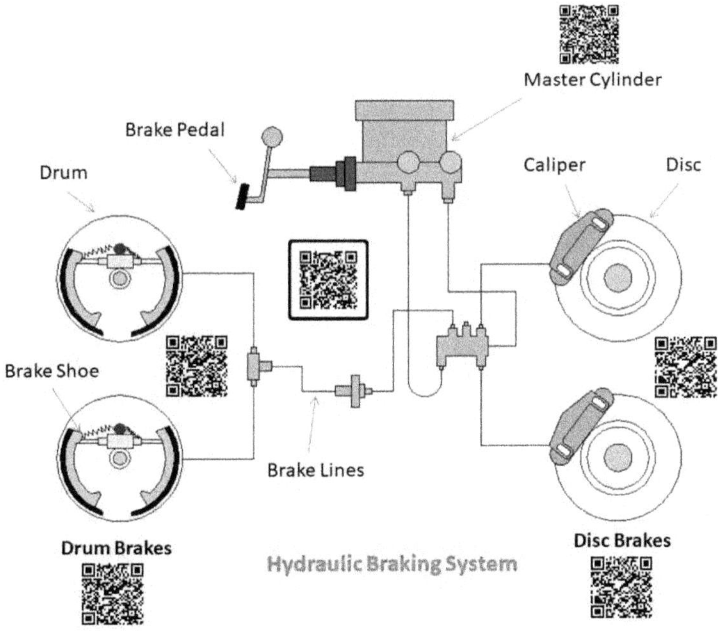
Master Cylinder
Brake Pedal
Drum
Caliper
Disc
Brake Shoe
Brake Lines
Drum Brakes
Hydraulic Braking System
Disc Brakes

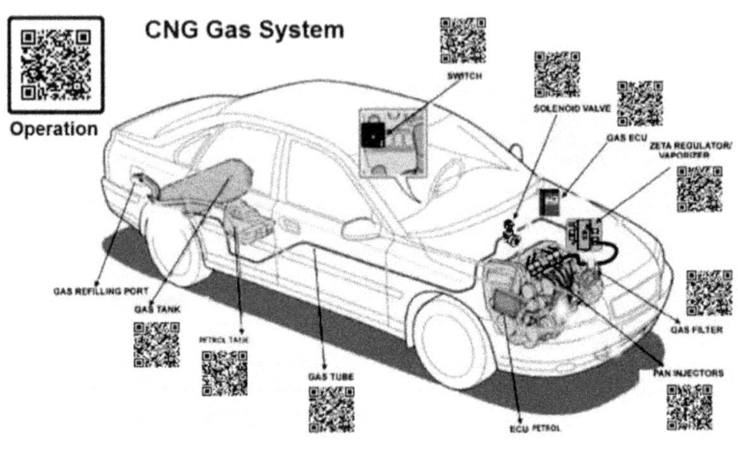
CNG Gas System
Operation
SWITCH
SOLENOID VALVE
GAS ECU
ZETA REGULATOR/ VAPORIZER
GAS REFILLING PORT
GAS TANK
GAS TUBE
GAS FILTER
PAN INJECTORS
ECU PETROL

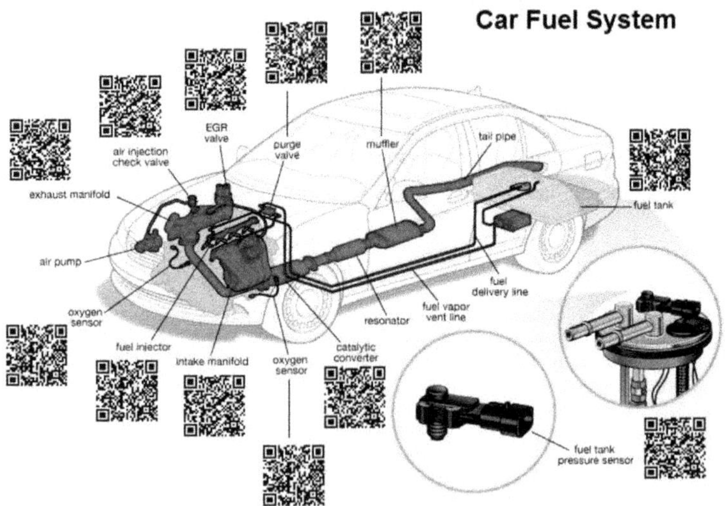
Car Fuel System
EGR valve
air injection check valve
purge valve
muffler
tail pipe
exhaust manifold
fuel tank
air pump
fuel delivery line
fuel vapor vent line
resonator
oxygen sensor
fuel injector
intake manifold
oxygen sensor
catalytic converter
fuel tank pressure sensor

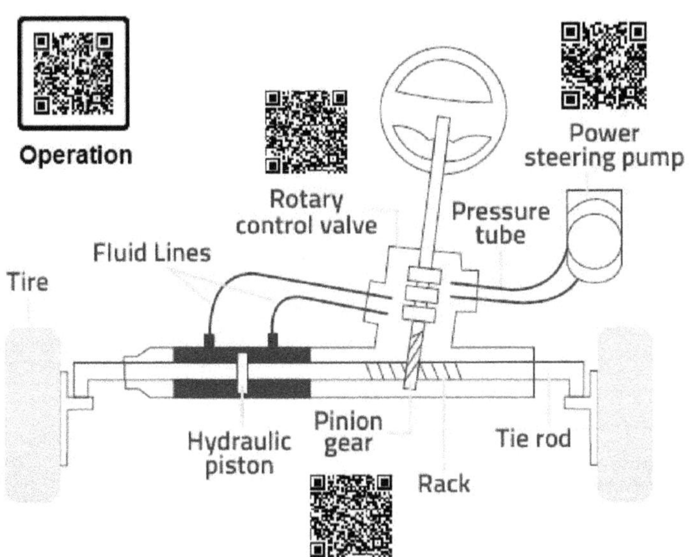

Power Steering System

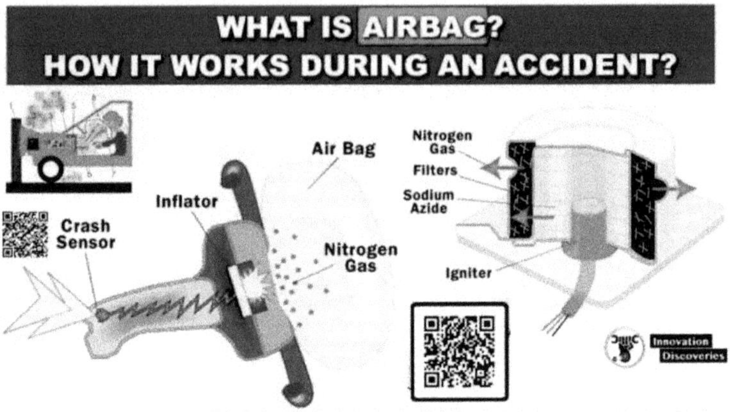

WHAT IS AIRBAG?
HOW IT WORKS DURING AN ACCIDENT?
Air Bag
Inflator
Crash Sensor
Nitrogen Gas
Nitrogen Gas
Filters
Sodium Azide
Igniter
Innovation Discoveries

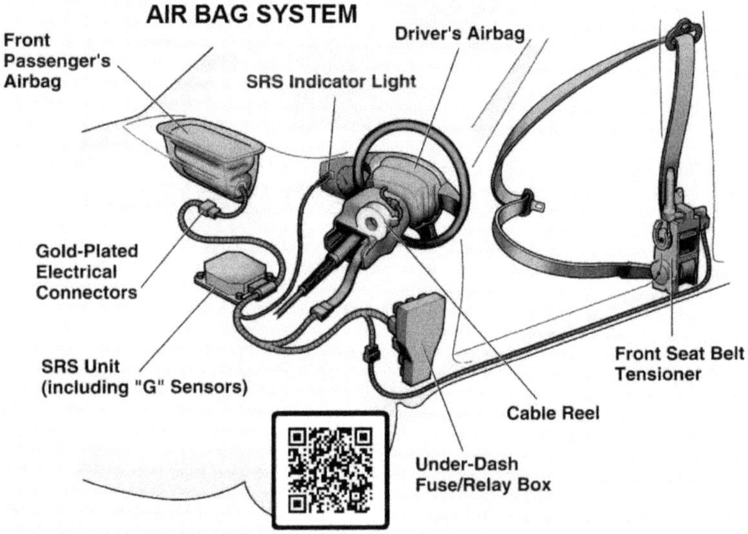

AIR BAG SYSTEM
Front Passenger's Airbag
Driver's Airbag
SRS Indicator Light
Gold-Plated Electrical Connectors
SRS Unit (including "G" Sensors)
Front Seat Belt Tensioner
Cable Reel
Under-Dash Fuse/Relay Box

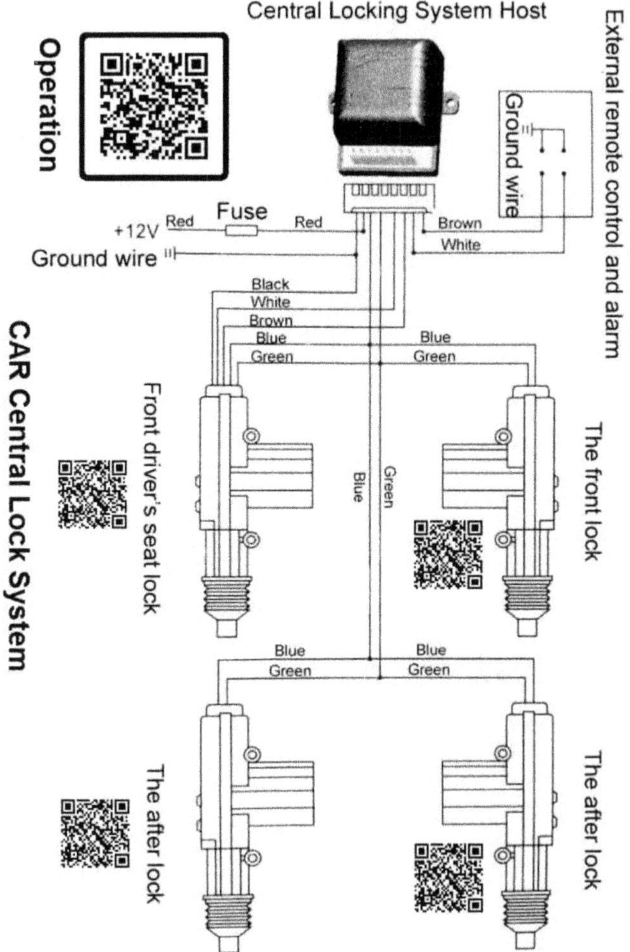
Central Locking System Host
External remote control and alarm
Ground wire
Operation
+12V
Red
Fuse
Red
Brown
White
Ground wire
Black
White
Brown
Blue
Green
Blue
Green
Green
Blue
CAR Central Lock System
Front driver's seat lock
The front lock
Blue
Green
Blue
Green
The after lock
The after lock

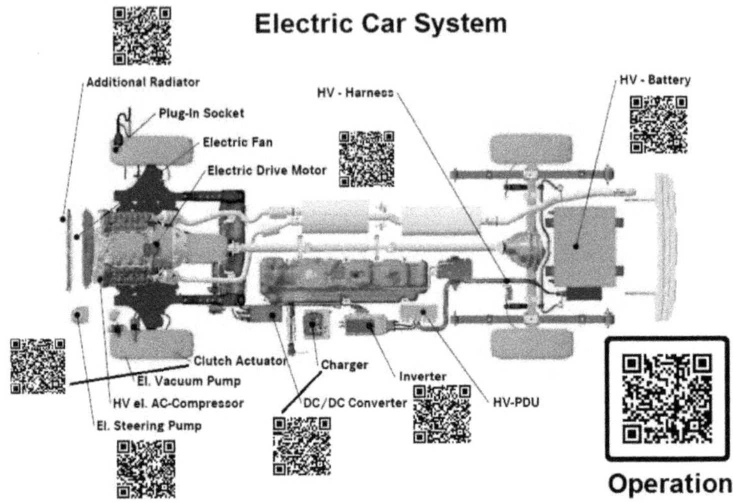

Multi Point Fuel Injection Syastem
D- MPFI & L- MPFI

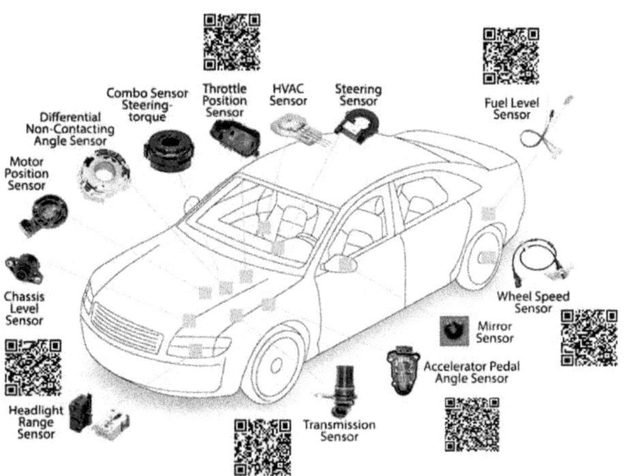

Car Sensor System

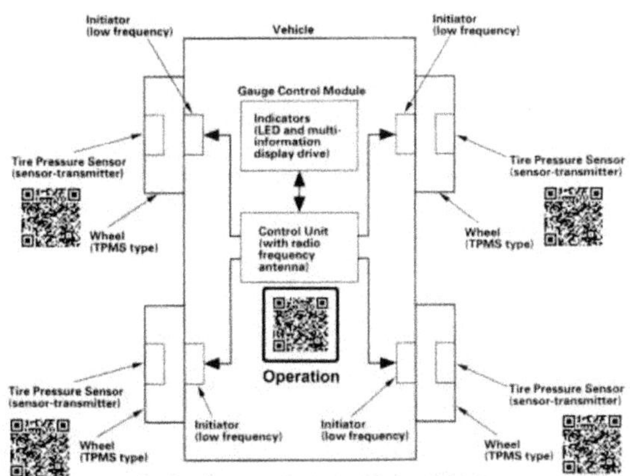

Car Tire Pressure Monitoring System (TPMS)

Dynamo (Alternator) distributor cap in car

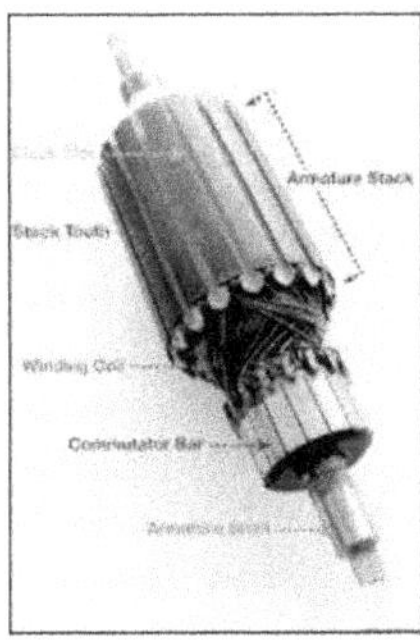

Starter winding armature in vehicle

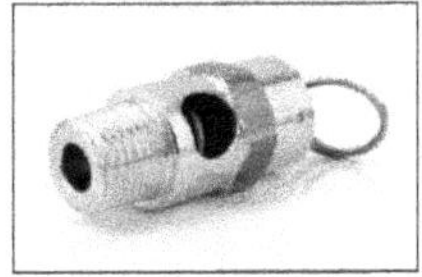

Air tank safety valve

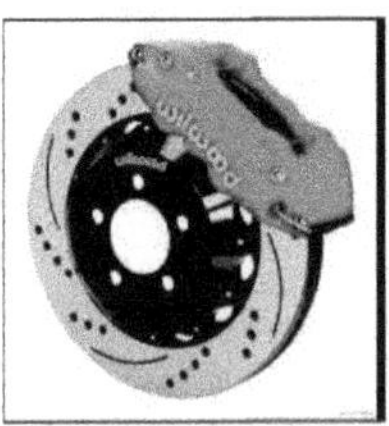

Brakes in car

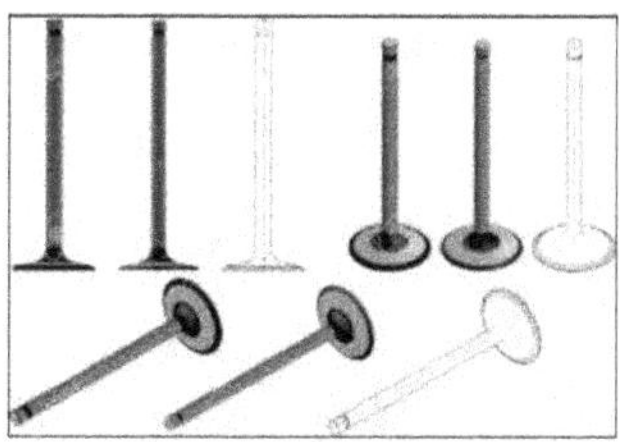

Engine valves

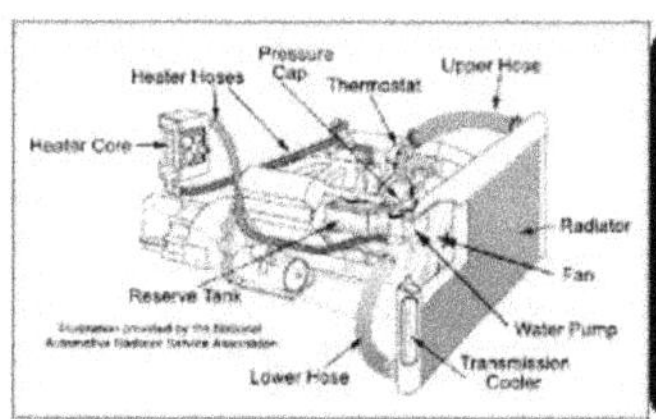

Cooling system in car

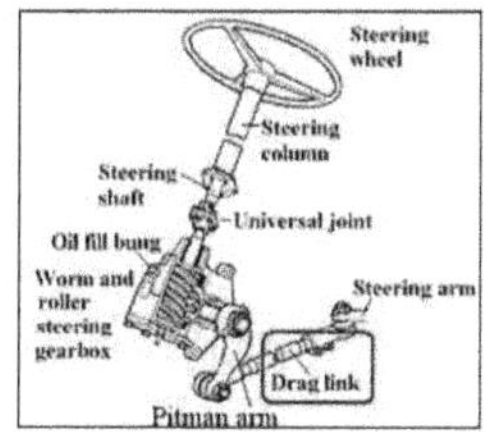

Steering gearbox in vehicle

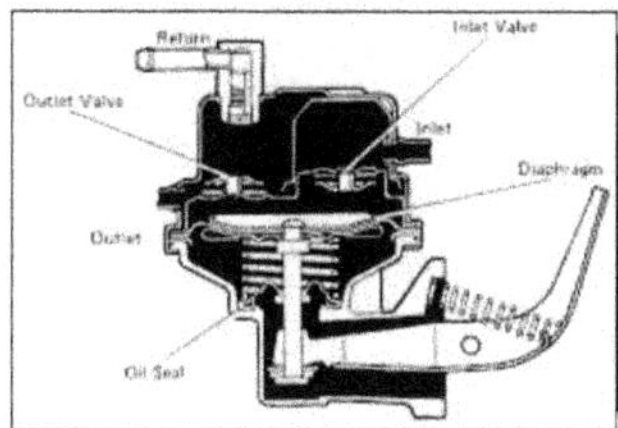

Fuel pump in Vehicle

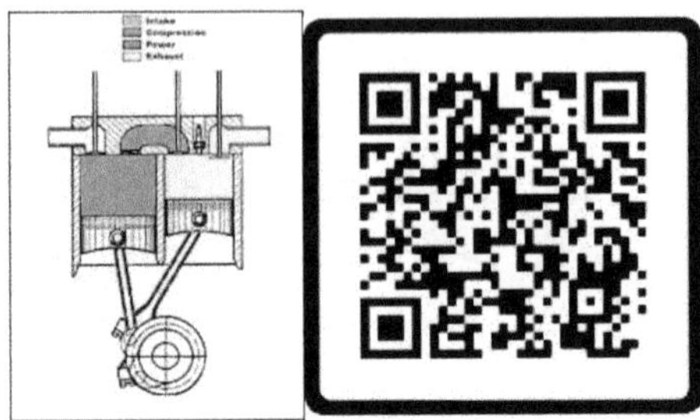

Engine in vehicle

Lead acid battery in vehicle

Piston & rings in Engine

Radiator cap in vehicle

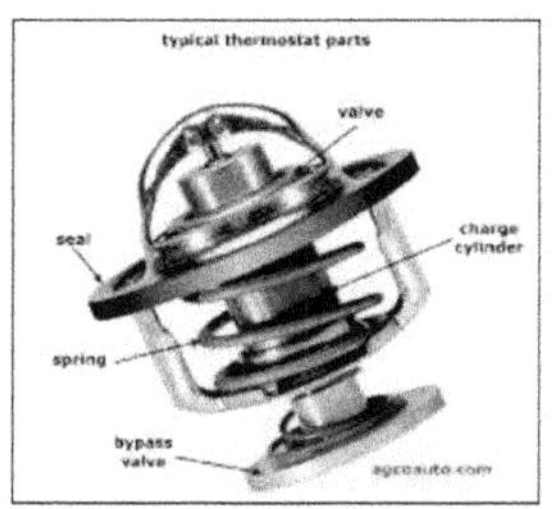

Thermostat valve in vehicle

CHAPTER TWO

Automobile Engineering Drawing Theory

Grinding

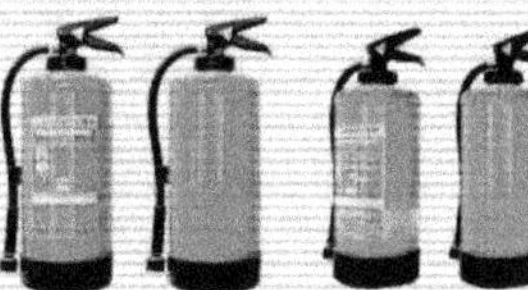

Fire extinguisher

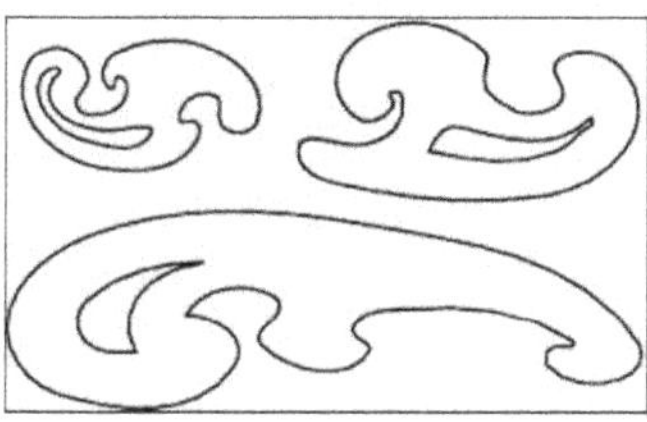

French curve in drawing

Set square in drawing

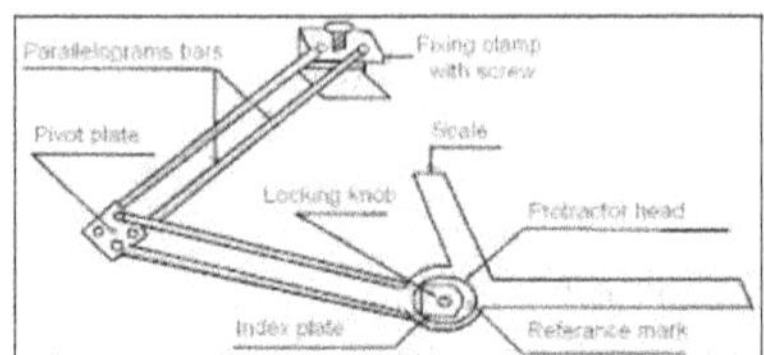

Mini drafter in drawing

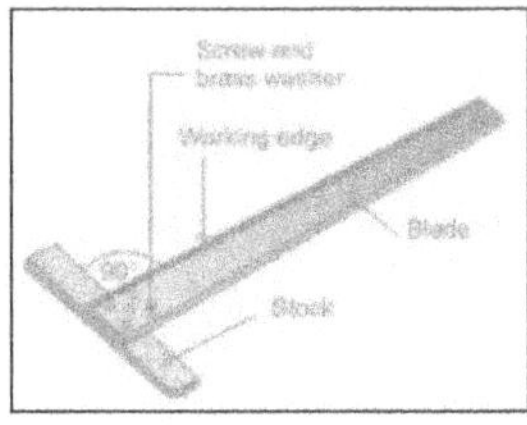

T - square in drawing

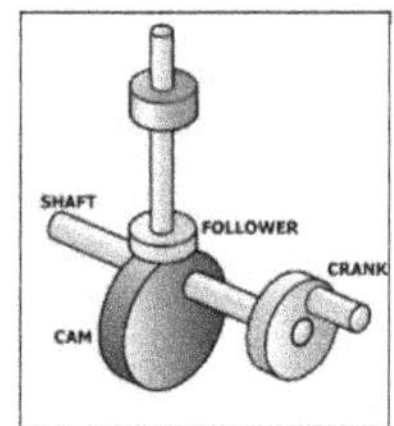

Cams in engine

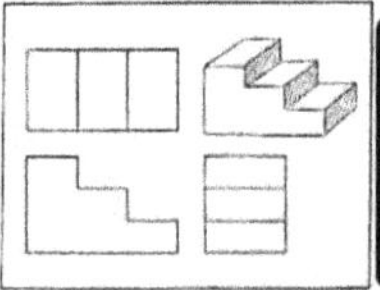

Orthographic projection in drawing

Third angle projection drawing

Cone in engineering drawing

Sphere in drawing

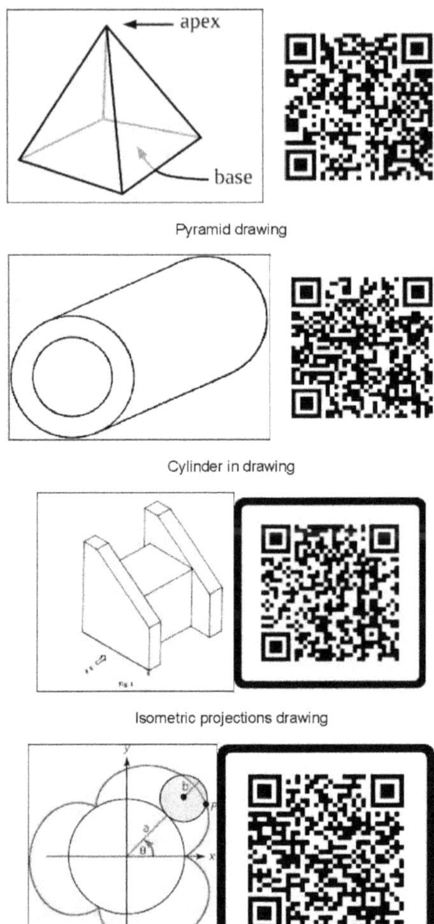

Pyramid drawing

Cylinder in drawing

Isometric projections drawing

Curves engineering drawing

Sectional views in drawing

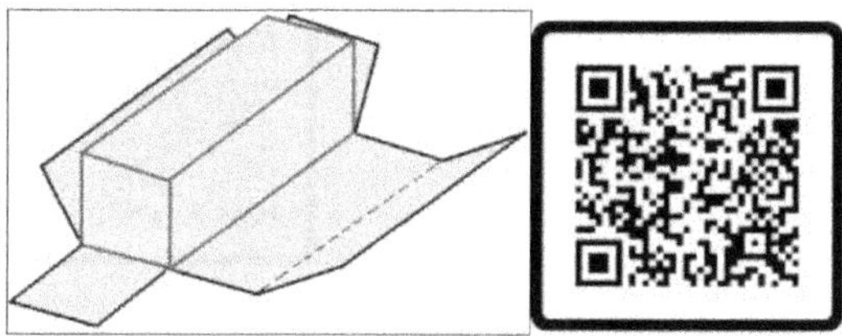

Development of surfaces in drawing

Hexagonal plane in drawing

Polyhedron in drawing

First Angle projection method in drawing

Springs in drawing

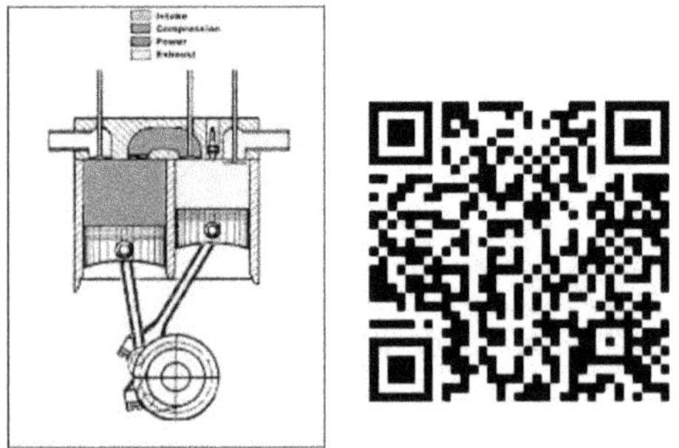

Engine in vehicle

CHAPTER THREE

Automobile Engineering AutoCAD Theory

AutoCAD Command Shortcut Keys

CTRL+Q	Exit public consciousness
CTRL+R	Remove ornamentation
CTRL+S	Save as Stainless Steel
CTRL+SHFT+S	Save as a better design (ie. Titanium)
CTRL+T	Toggles Talent (requires administrative access)
CTRL+V	Value Engineer (reduces scale by 78%)
CTRL+SHFT+V	Pastes data from ArchRecord as Block
CTRL+X	Begin unpaid Furlough
CTRL+Y	Repeats last award winning design
CTRL+Z	Speed dial Zaha Hadid
CTRL+ZZZ	Sleep (not applicable)
CTRL+[	Cancels current schedule
CTRL+\	Cancels current budget
CTRL+ANGST+DEL	(no action)

F1	Displays Help wanted sign in café window
F2	Toggles all text to Helvetica
F3	Toggles Oh-SNAP
F4	Toggles MODERNISM
F5	Toggles ISOLATION
F6	Toggles CORBUSIER
F7	Toggles IRRELEVANT GRID
F8	Toggles ORTHO MODE (should always be on)
F9	Toggles POSTMODERNISM (should always be off)
F10	Toggles NORWAY
F11	Toggles ARROGANCE

AutoCAD Command Shortcut Keys

ALT+F8	Delete detail
ALT+F11	Add white
CTRL+1	Simplify Palette
CTRL+2	Remove Interior Design Palette
CTRL+3	Complicate Construction Process
CTRL+4	Add 4 extraneous sheets
CTRL+5	Remove Client's color Palette
CTRL+6	Remove Client's wife's color Palette (must press hard)
CTRL+7	Markup Set for interns (with only circles and question marks)
CTRL+A	Selects objects in drawing that aren't really needed
CTRL+B	Sends resume to B.I.G.
CTRL+SHIFT+B	Shifts blame to Consultants
CTRL+C	Copies angst to Clipboard
CTRL+SHFT+C	Copies angst to Clipboard with Base Point (ie. Finland)
CTRL+D	Delete relevance
CTRL+E	Cycles through design ideologies
CTRL+F	Flatten all roofs
CTRL+G	Insert 9-square Grid
CTRL+H	Insert Awesomeness
CTRL+L	Adds "Le" in front of all nouns
CTRL+K	Justify design concept
CTRL+L	Left justify design concept
CTRL+M	Less and/or more
CTRL+N	Insert new idea (bills client for additional time required)
CTRL+O	Opens ArchDaily.com
CTRL+P	Prints unemployment check

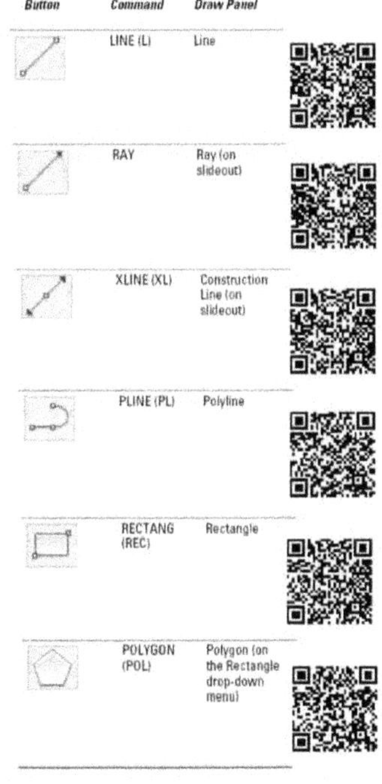

Button	Command	Draw Panel
	LINE (L)	Line
	RAY	Ray (on slideout)
	XLINE (XL)	Construction Line (on slideout)
	PLINE (PL)	Polyline
	RECTANG (REC)	Rectangle
	POLYGON (POL)	Polygon (on the Rectangle drop-down menu)

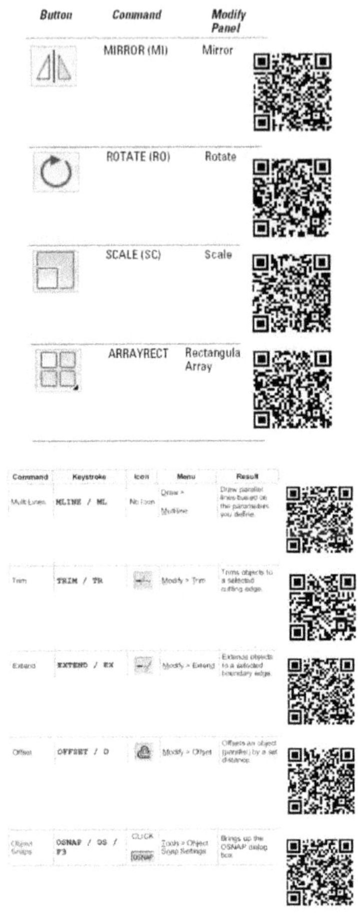

Button	Command	Modify Panel
	MIRROR (MI)	Mirror
	ROTATE (RO)	Rotate
	SCALE (SC)	Scale
	ARRAYRECT	Rectangula Array

Command	Keystroke	Icon	Menu	Result
Multi Lines	MLINE / ML	No Icon	Draw > Multline	Draw parallel lines based on the parameters you define.
Trim	TRIM / TR		Modify > Trim	Trims objects to a selected cutting edge.
Extend	EXTEND / EX		Modify > Extend	Extends objects to a selected boundary edge.
Offset	OFFSET / O		Modify > Offset	Offsets an object (parallel) by a set distance.
Object Snaps	OSNAP / OS / F3	CLICK OSNAP	Tools > Object Snap Settings	Brings up the OSNAP dialog box.

Command	Menu
EXTEND (EX)	Extend (on drop-down button)
LENGTHEN (LEN)	Lengthen (on slideout panel)
BREAK (BR), two points	Break (on slideout panel)
BREAK (BR), 1 point	Break at point (on slideout panel)
EXPLODE (X)	Explode
FILLET (F)	Fillet (on drop-down button)

Command	Keystroke	Icon	Menu	Result
Line	Line / L		Draw > Line	Draws a straight line segment from one point to the next
Circle	Circle / C		Draw > Circle > Center, Radius	Draws a circle based on a center point and radius
Erase	Erase / E		Modify > Erase	Erases an object
Print	Print / Plot Cntl+P		File > Print	Enables the Print/Plot Configuration Dialog Box
Undo	U (Don't use 'Undo' for now)		Edit > Undo	Undoes the last command
Rectangle	RECTANGLE / REC		Draw > Rectangle	Draws a rectangle after you enter one corner and then the second.

Button	Command	Modify Panel
	ERASE (E)	Erase
	MOVE (M)	Move
	COPY (CO or CP)	Copy
	STRETCH (S)	Stretch
	ARRAYPOLAR	Polar Array
	ARRAYPATH	Path Array
	ARRAYEDIT	Edit Array (on slideout panel)
	OFFSET (O)	Offset
	TRIM (TR)	Trim (on drop-down button)

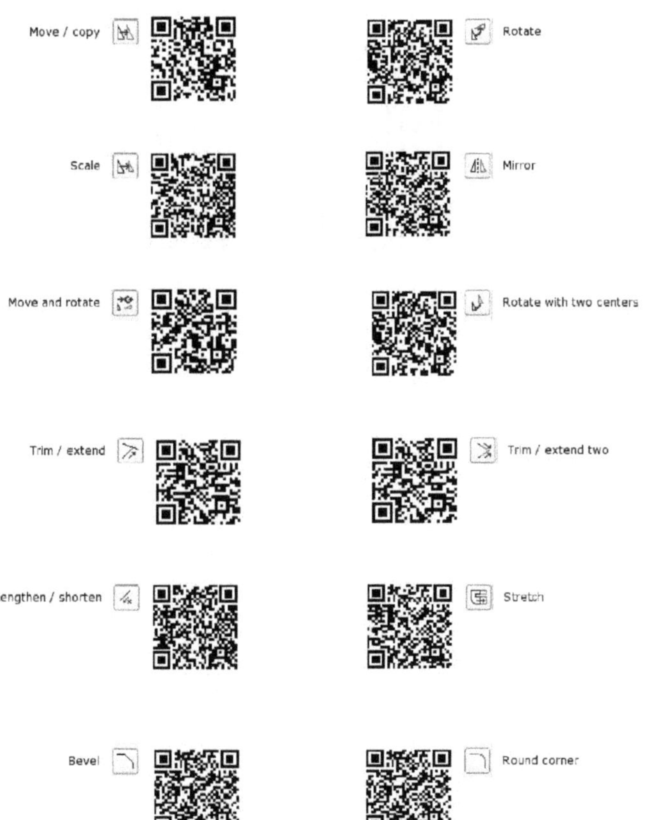
Move / copy
Rotate
Scale
Mirror
Move and rotate
Rotate with two centers
Trim / extend
Trim / extend two
Lengthen / shorten
Stretch
Bevel
Round corner

CHAPTER FOUR

Automobile Engineering Electrical Theory

14 ITI Book MCQ - Manoj Dole
www.itibook.com
battery
capacitor
cell
dynamometer
electromagnet
heater
inductance
magnet
www.itigov.blogspot.com www.jobapprentices.blogspot.com www.ititests.blogspot.com
www.itibook.com

35 ITI Book MCQ - Manoj Dole
www.itibook.com
megger
motor
multimeter
ohmmeter
resistores
star connected
alternator
voltmeter
ammeter
wattmeter
www.itigov.blogspot.com www.jobapprentices.blogspot.com www.ititests.blogspot.com
www.itibook.com

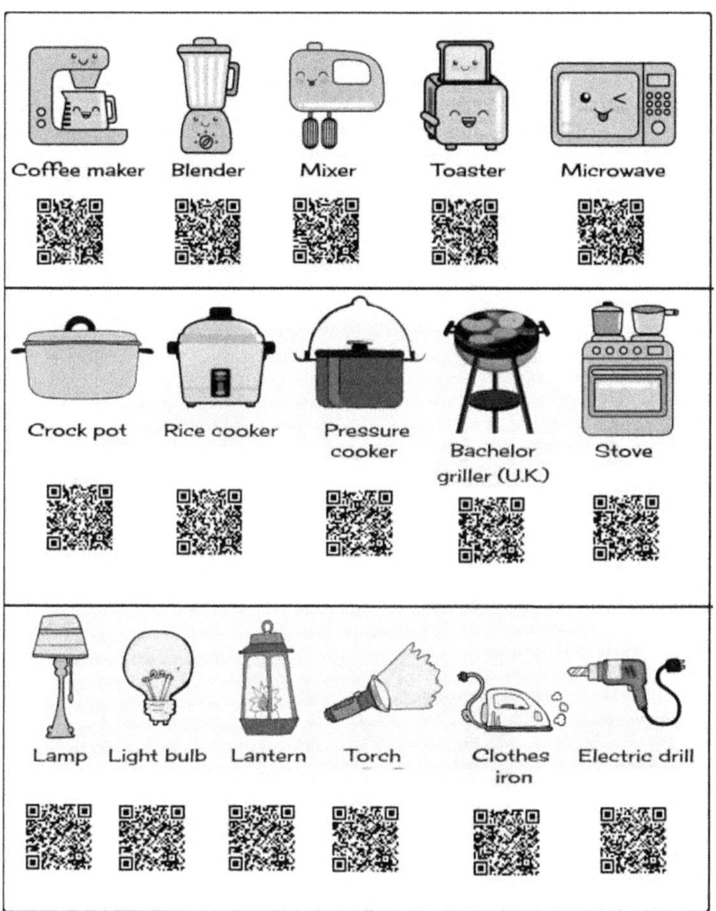
Coffee maker
Blender
Mixer
Toaster
Microwave
Crock pot
Rice cooker
Pressure cooker
Bachelor griller (U.K.)
Stove
Lamp
Light bulb
Lantern
Torch
Clothes iron
Electric drill

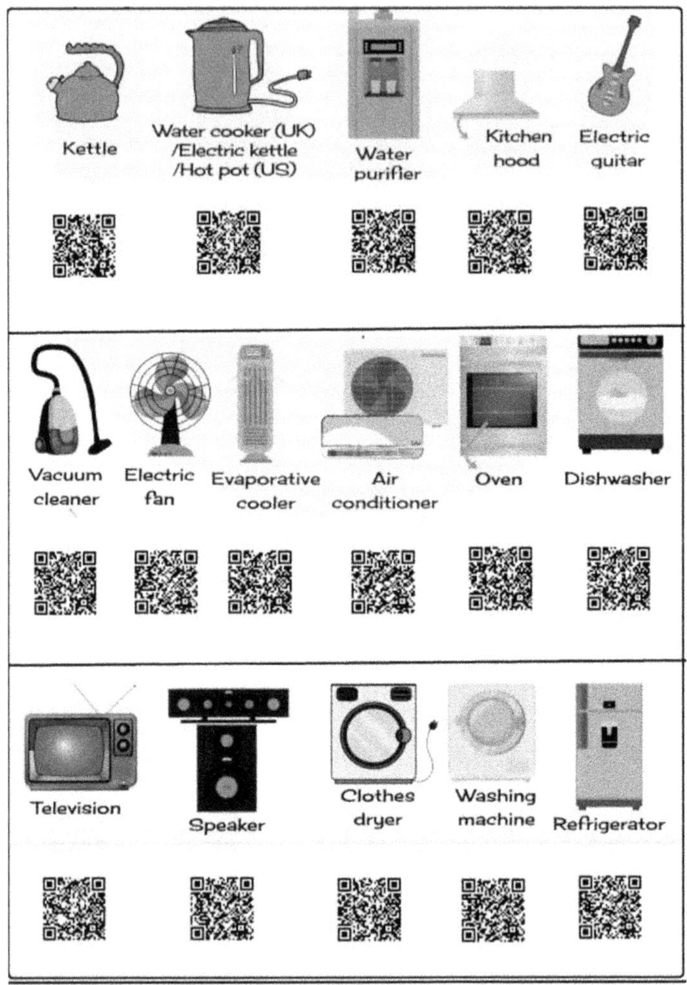
Kettle
Water cooker (UK)
/Electric kettle
/Hot pot (US)
Water
purifier
Kitchen
hood
Electric
guitar
Vacuum
cleaner
Electric
fan
Evaporative
cooler
Air
conditioner
Oven
Dishwasher
Television
Speaker
Clothes
dryer
Washing
machine
Refrigerator

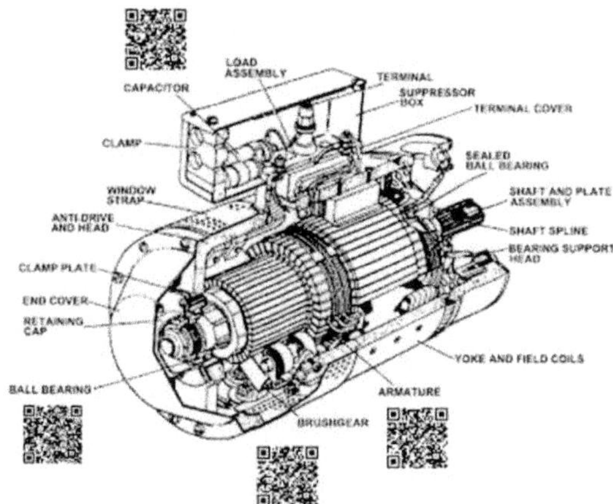

Electrical Generator

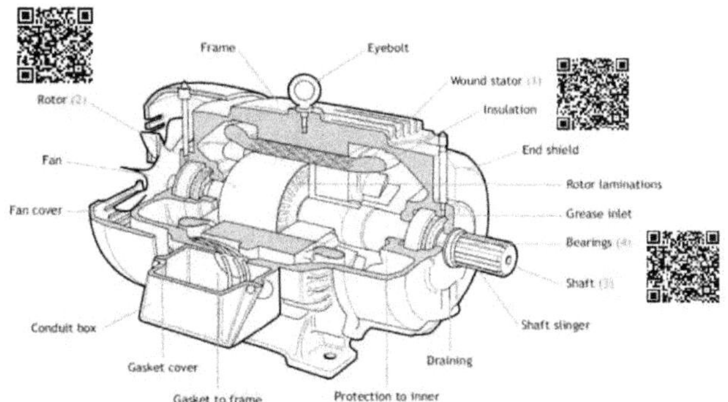

Electrical Induction Motor

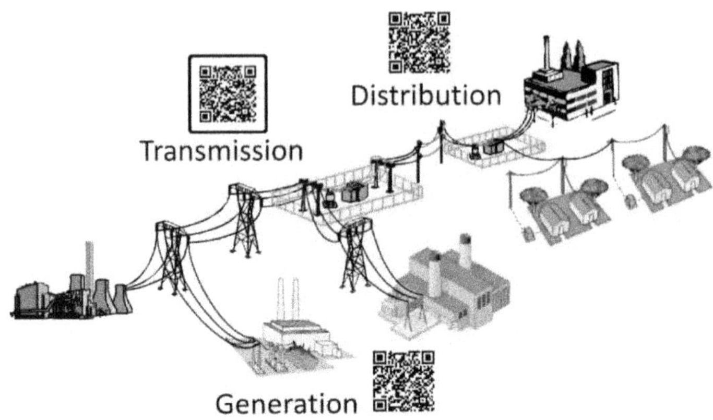

Electrical Power Distribution

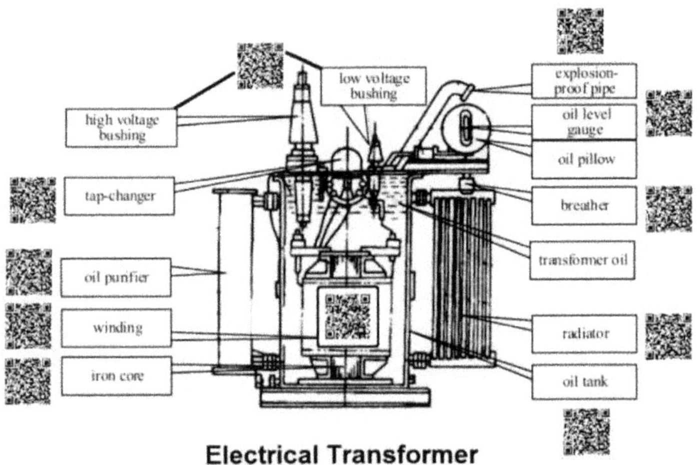

Electrical Transformer

CHAPTER FIVE

Automobile Engineering Hydraulic & Pnumatic Theory

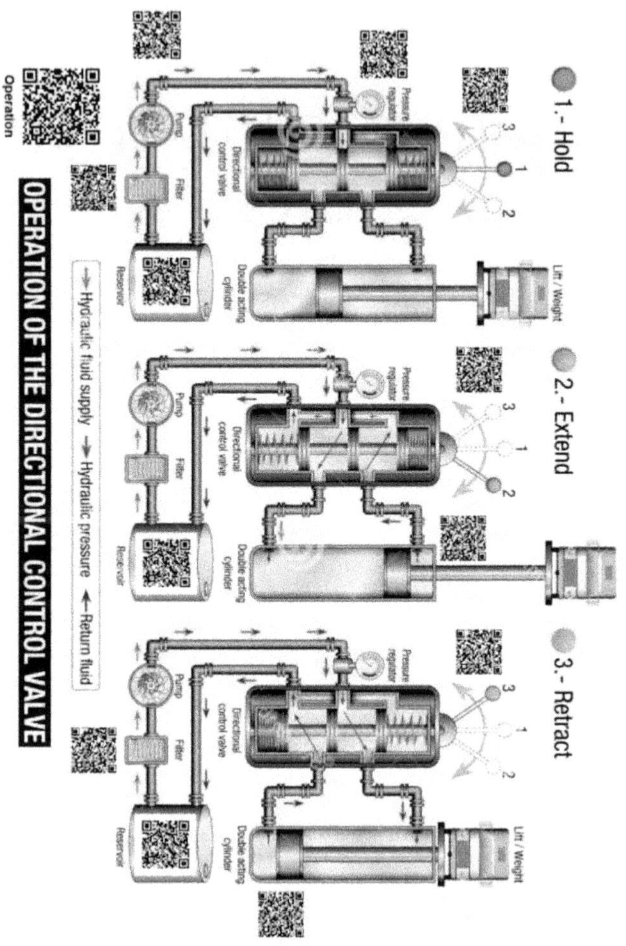
1.- Hold
2.- Extend
3.- Retract
Pressure regulator
Directional control valve
Pump
Filter
Reservoir
Double acting cylinder
Lift / Weight
Hydraulic fluid supply
Hydraulic pressure
Return fluid
OPERATION OF THE DIRECTIONAL CONTROL VALVE
Operation

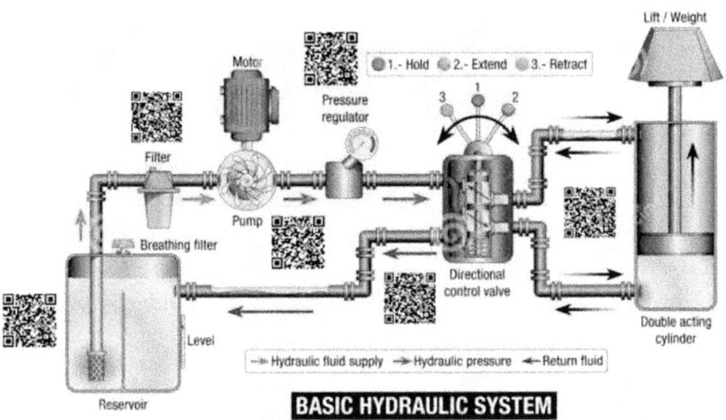

Direct Pressure Relief Valves

- The pressure relief valve provides protection against overload experienced by the actuators in a hydraulic system. One important function is to limit the force or torque produced by the hydraulic cylinders or motors.

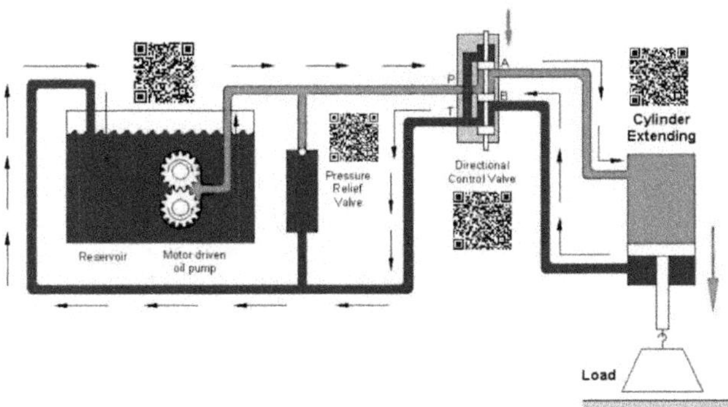

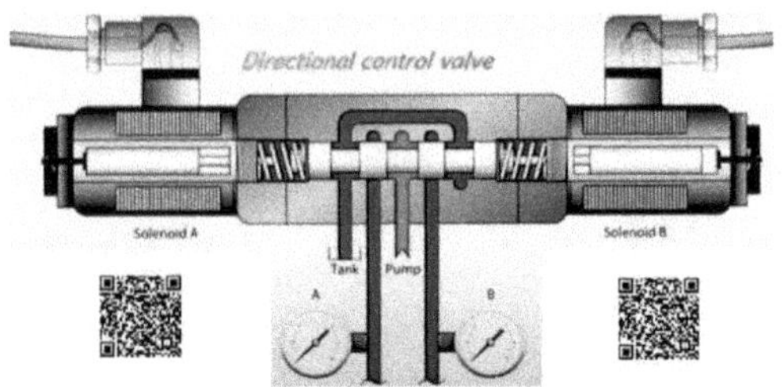

Double Acting, Single ended Cylinder

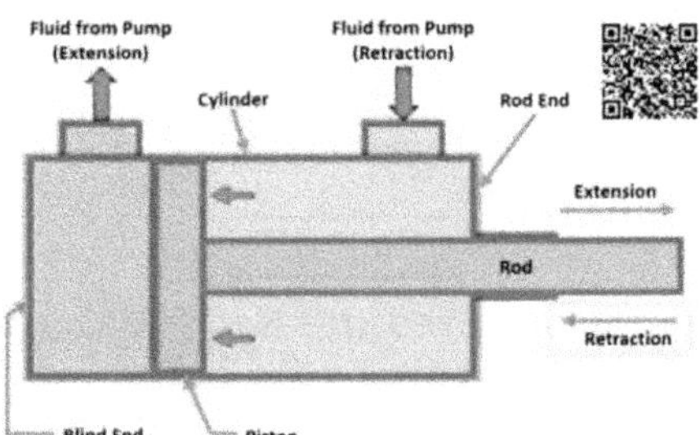

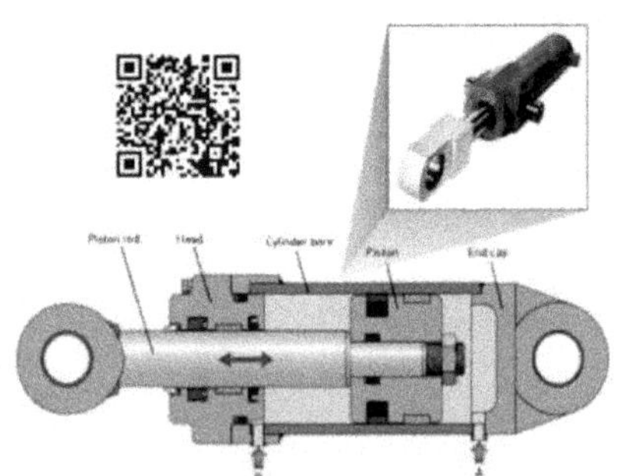

Hydraulic Cylinder

FLOW CONTROL VALVES

- A flow control valve can regulate the flow or pressure of the fluid.
- The fluid flow is controlled by varying area of the valve opening through which fluid passes.

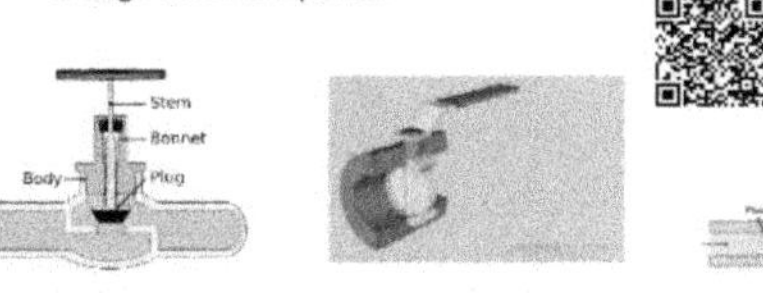

GLOBE VALVE BUTTERFLY VALVE PLUG VALVE

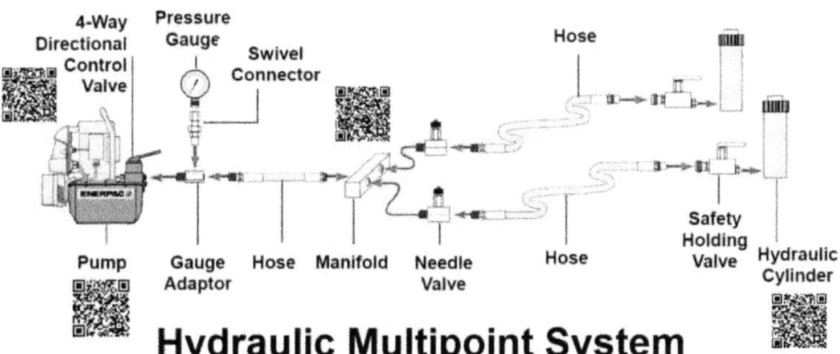

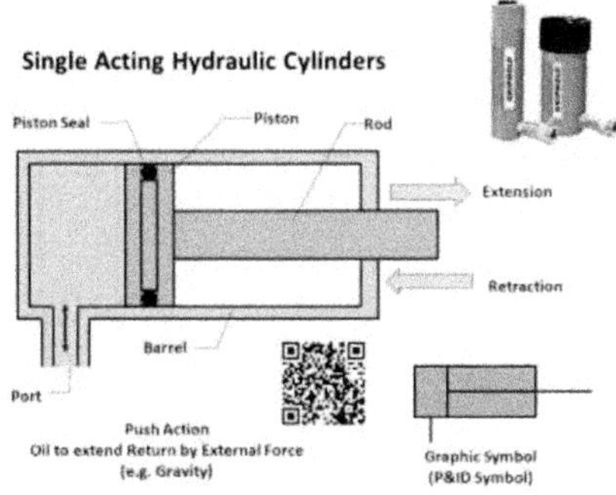

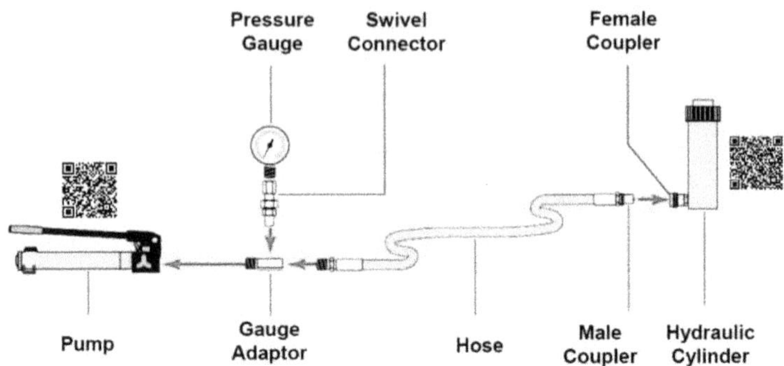

Hydraulic Single Point System

Types of Hydraulic Valves

- **Directional Control Valve:**
  Control the direction of flow of the hydraulic fluid to different lines in the circuit

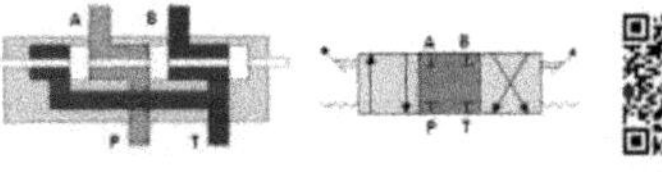

- **Flow Control Valves:**
  Control the amount of fluid flow in the circuit

- **Pressure Control Valves:**
  Control the pressure in different segments in the circuit

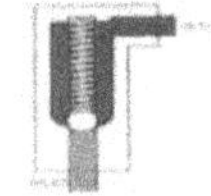

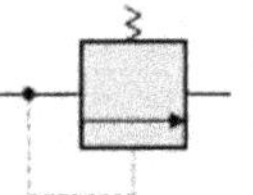

Hydraulic Valves - Parts and Components

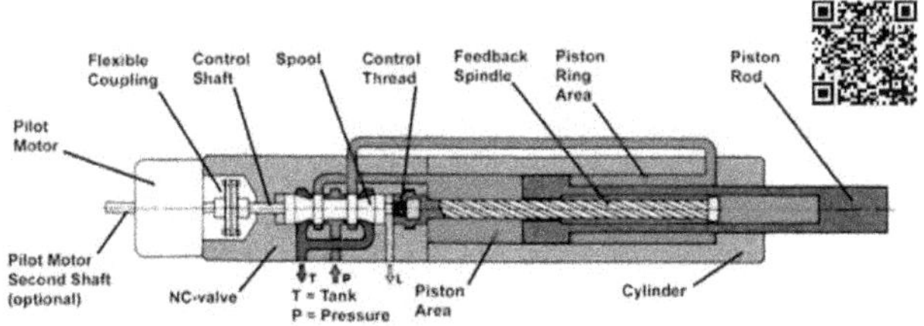

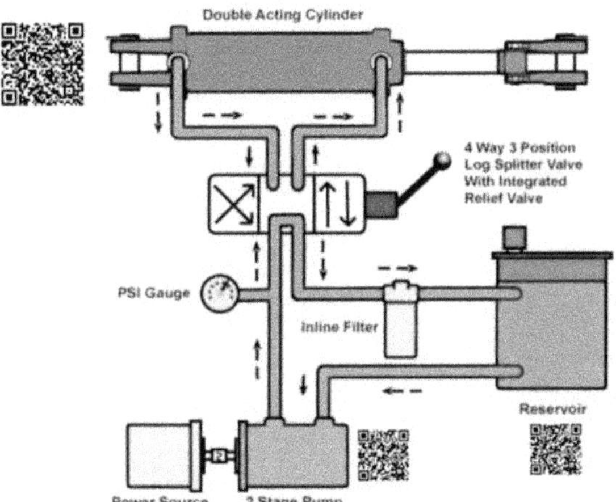

Hydraulic Double Acting Cylinder

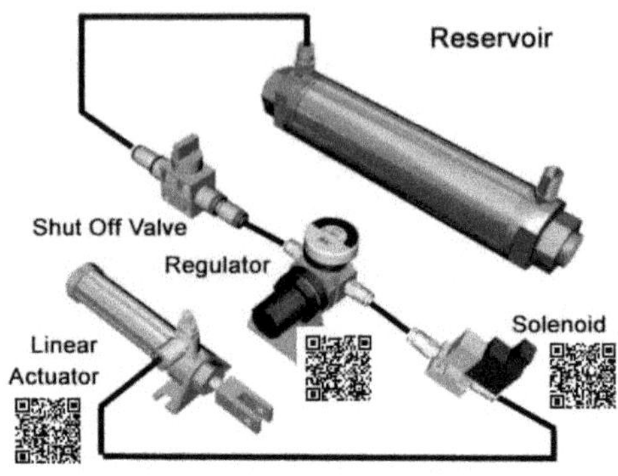

Pneumatic System

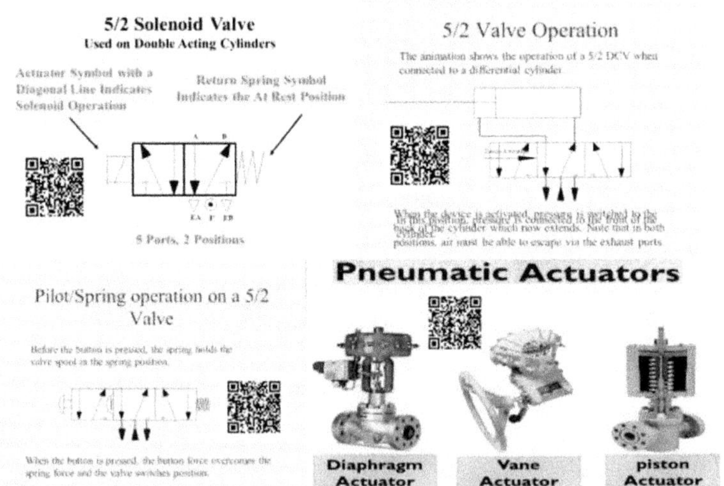

Pneumatic Control Valve

Pneumatic Control Valve Mechanisem

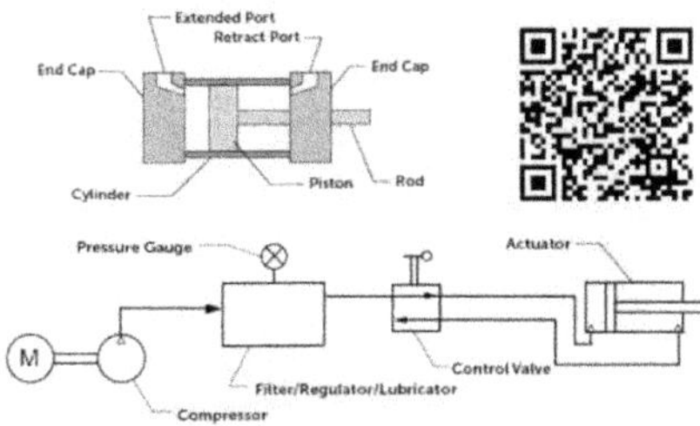

Pneumatic Cylinder System

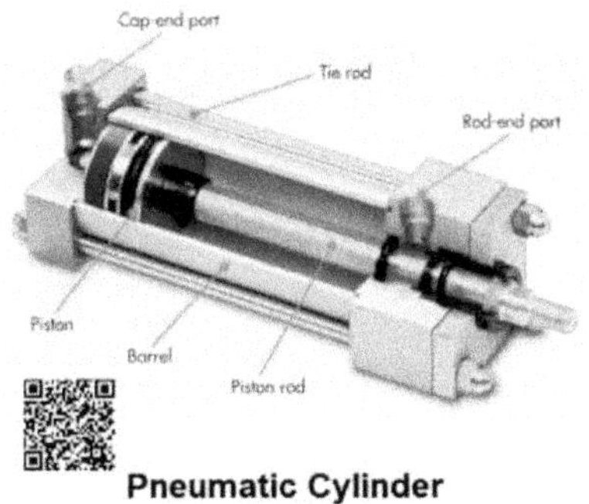

Pneumatic Cylinder

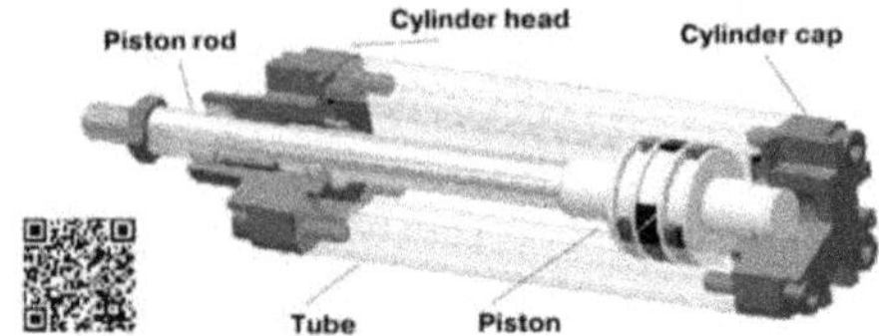
Pneumatic Cylinder
Piston rod
Cylinder head
Cylinder cap
Tube
Piston

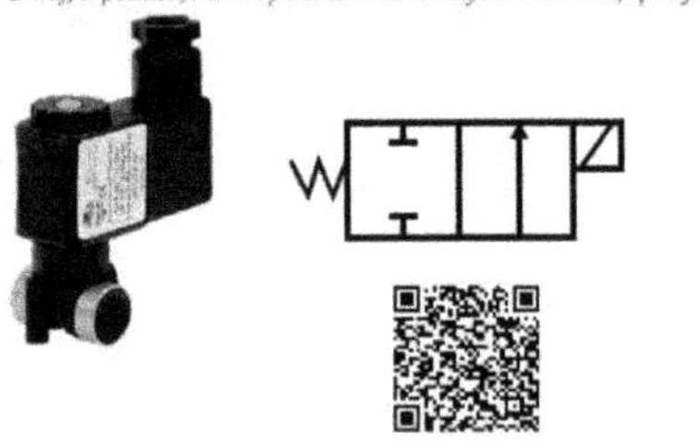
2-way, 2-position, normally closed direct-acting solenoid valve, spring return

4-way (5-port), 2-position, piloted solenoid valve, spring return
A B
R P S

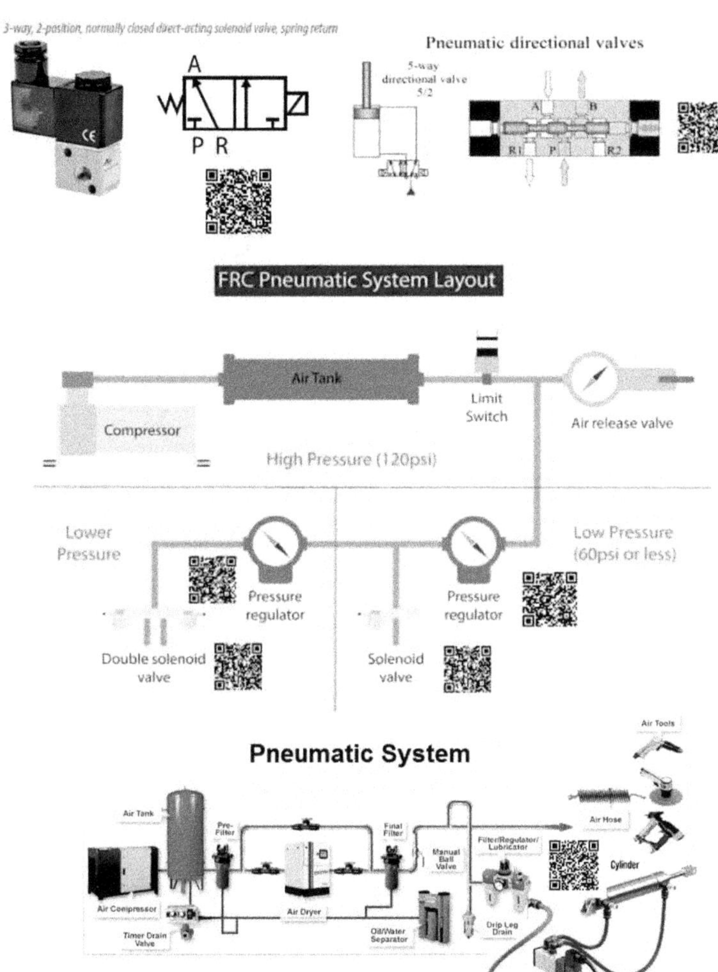
3-way, 2-position, normally closed direct-acting solenoid valve, spring return
A
P R
Pneumatic directional valves
5-way directional valve 5/2
A B
R1 P R2
FRC Pneumatic System Layout
Air Tank
Limit Switch
Air release valve
Compressor
High Pressure (120psi)
Lower Pressure
Low Pressure (60psi or less)
Pressure regulator
Pressure regulator
Double solenoid valve
Solenoid valve
Pneumatic System
Air Tools
Air Tank
Pre-Filter
Final Filter
Air Hose
Filter/Regulator/Lubricator
Manual Ball Valve
Cylinder
Air Compressor
Air Dryer
Timer Drain Valve
Oil/Water Separator
Drip Leg Drain
Valve

CHAPTER SIX

Automobile Engineering Welding Theory

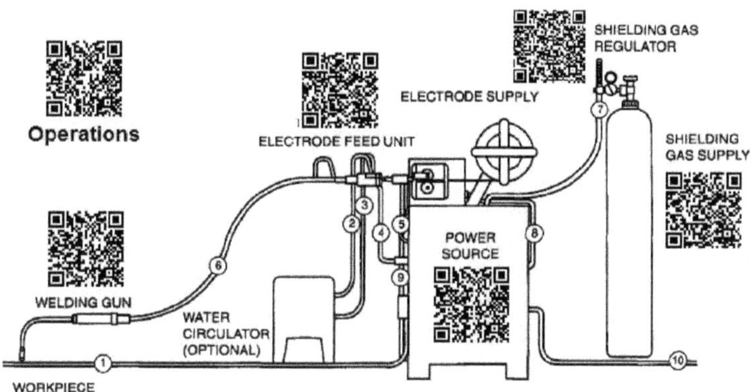

Gas Metal Arc Welding

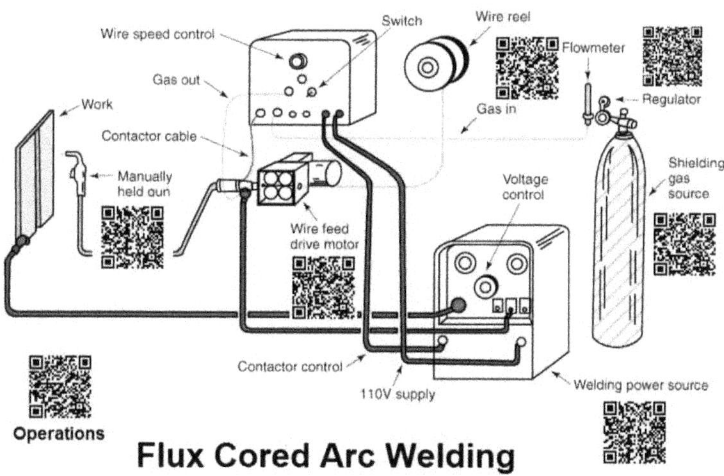

Flux Cored Arc Welding

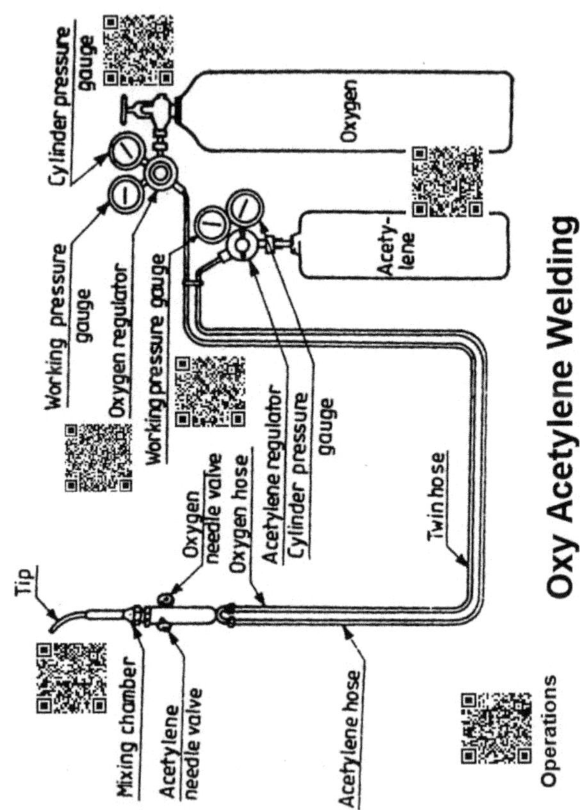
Cylinder pressure gauge
Oxygen
Working pressure gauge
Oxygen regulator
Working pressure gauge
Acety-lene
Acetylene regulator
Cylinder pressure gauge
Twin hose
Tip
Oxygen needle valve
Oxygen hose
Mixing chamber
Acetylene needle valve
Acetylene hose
Operations
Oxy Acetylene Welding

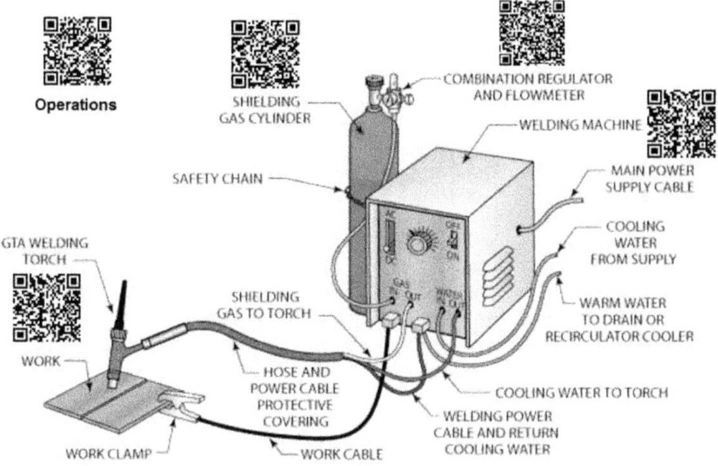

GTAW EQUIPMENT
(GAS TUNGSTEN ARC WELDING)

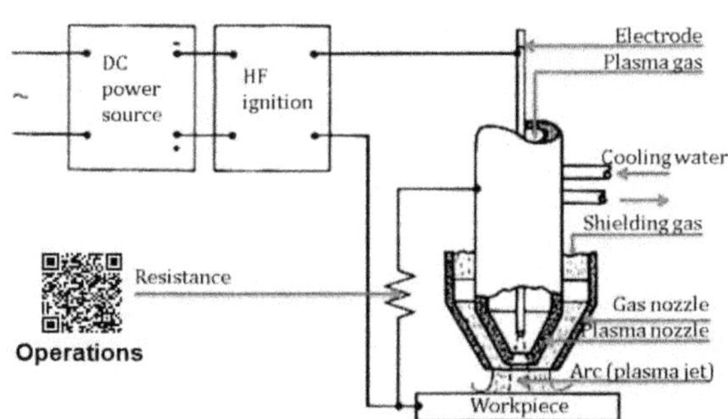

Plasma Transferred Arc Welding

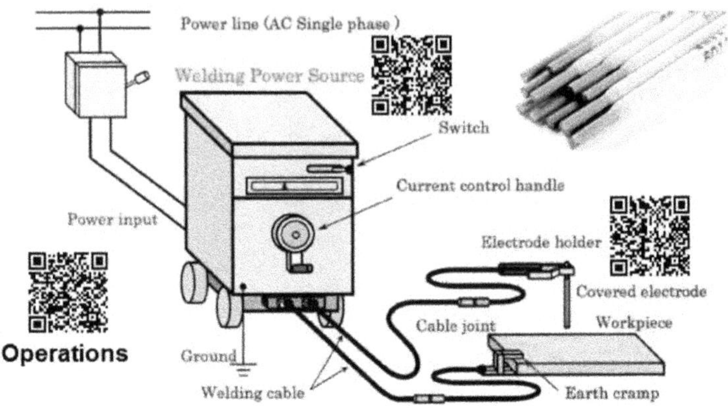

Shielded Metal Arc Welding

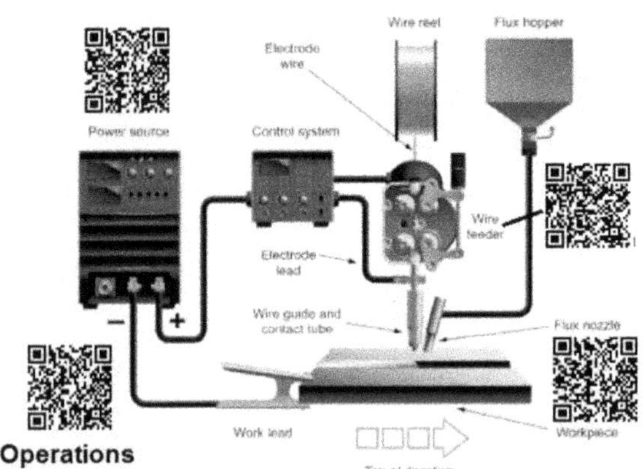

Submerged Arc Welding

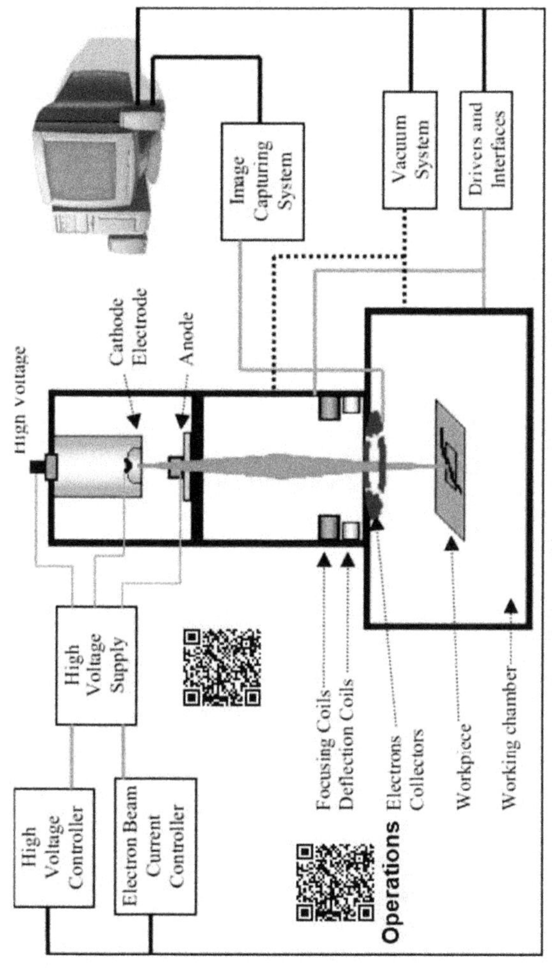
High Voltage
Cathode Electrode
Anode
High Voltage Controller
Electron Beam Current Controller
High Voltage Supply
Image Capturing System
Vacuum System
Drivers and Interfaces
Operations
Focusing Coils
Deflection Coils
Electrons Collectors
Workpiece
Working chamber
Electron Energy Beam Welding

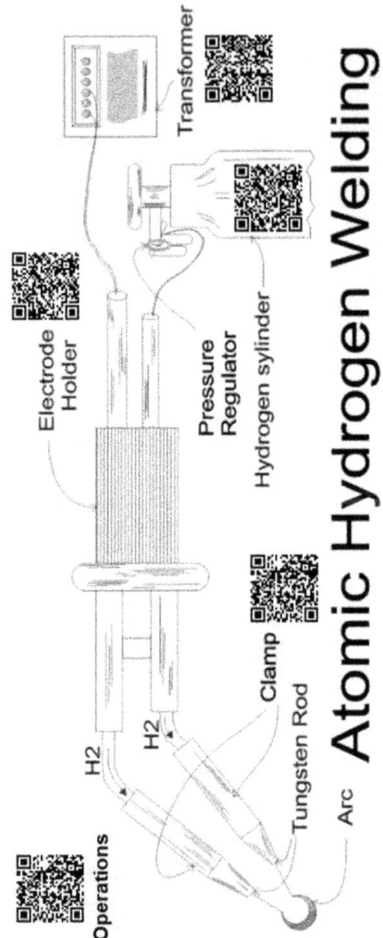
Transformer
Electrode
Holder
Pressure
Regulator
Hydrogen sylinder
Clamp
Tungsten Rod
Arc
H2
H2
Operations
Atomic Hydrogen Welding

nibbling machine

slant notch

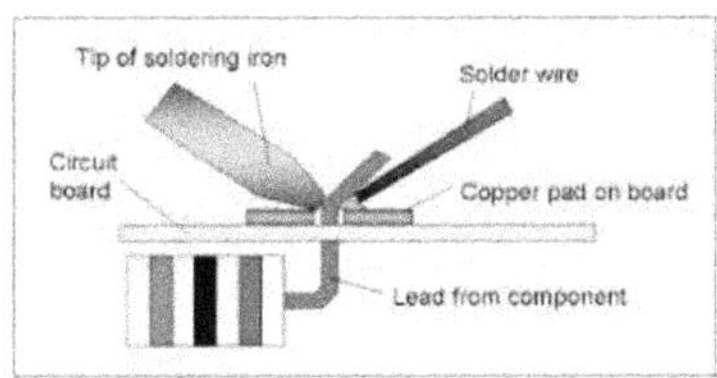

soldering

acytiline gas purifier

hydraulic back pressure valve

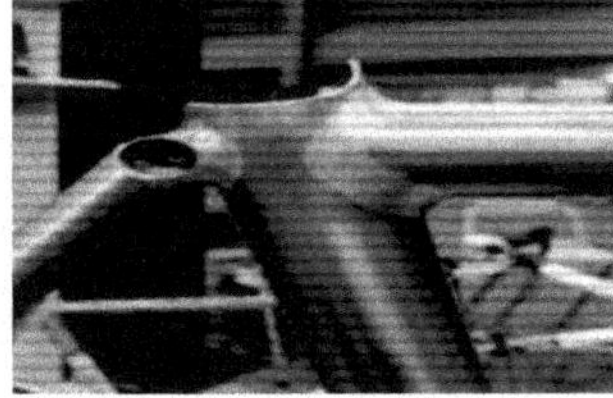

bronze welding

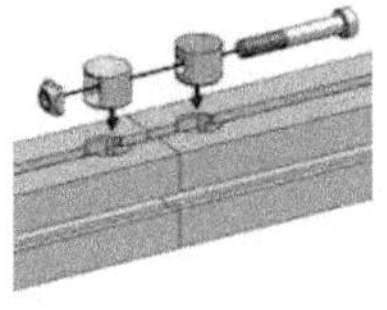

aluminium butt joint

coated electrodes

dc welding generator

nick break test

pipe welding

welding joints

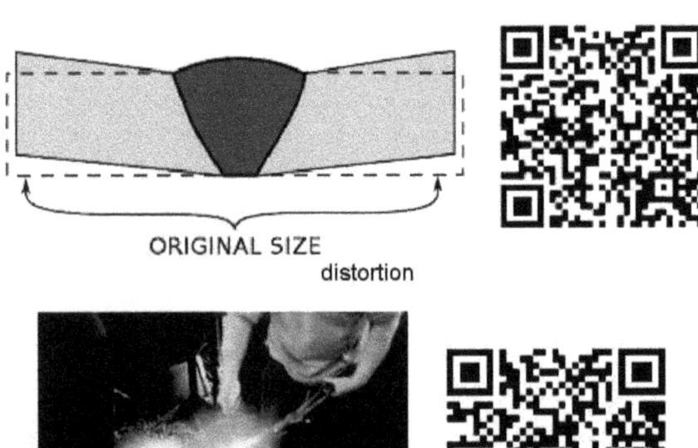

distortion

forge welding

residual stresses

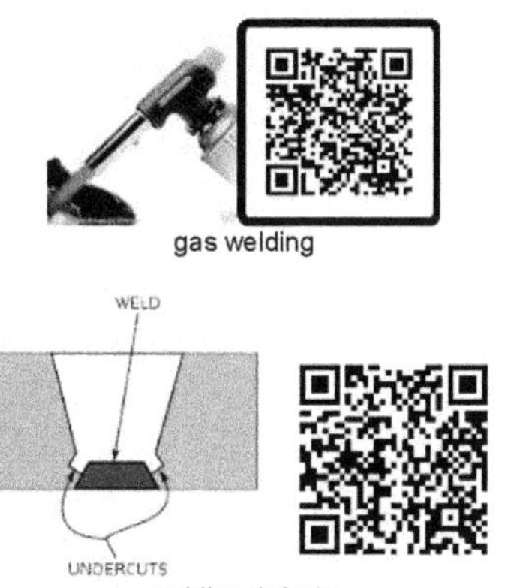

gas welding

welding defects

Enter Caption

CHAPTER SEVEN

Automobile Engineering Sheet Metal Work Theory

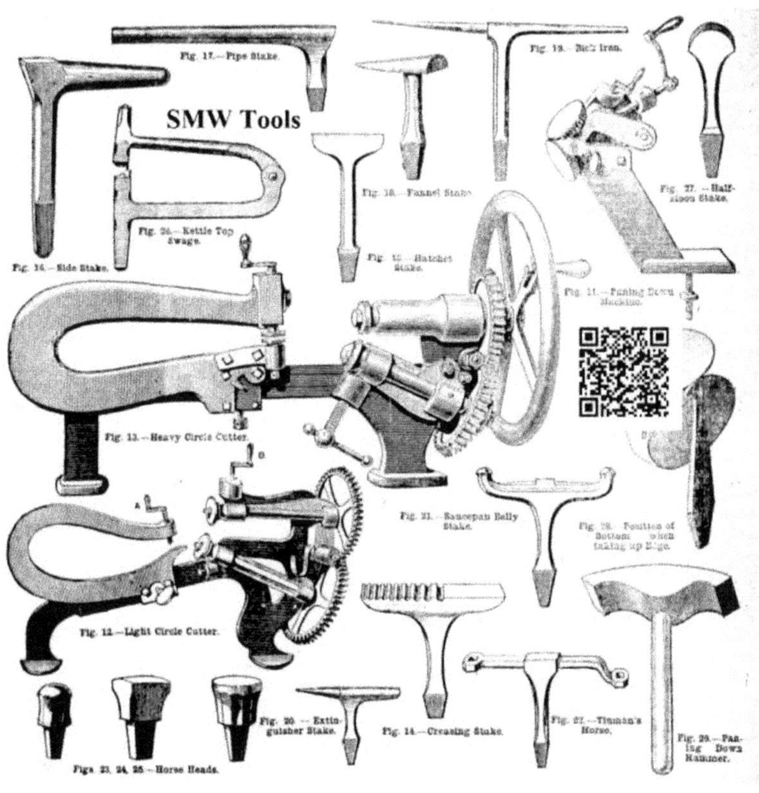
SMW Tools
Fig. 17.—Pipe Stake.
Fig. 16.—Side Stake.
Fig. 26.—Kettle Top Swage.
Hatchet Stake.
Fig. 13.—Heavy Circle Cutter.
Fig. 12.—Light Circle Cutter.
Fig. 21.—Saucepan Belly Stake.
Figs. 23, 24, 25.—Horse Heads.
Fig. 20.—Extinguisher Stake.
Fig. 14.—Creasing Stake.
Tinman's Horse.
Paning Down Hammer.

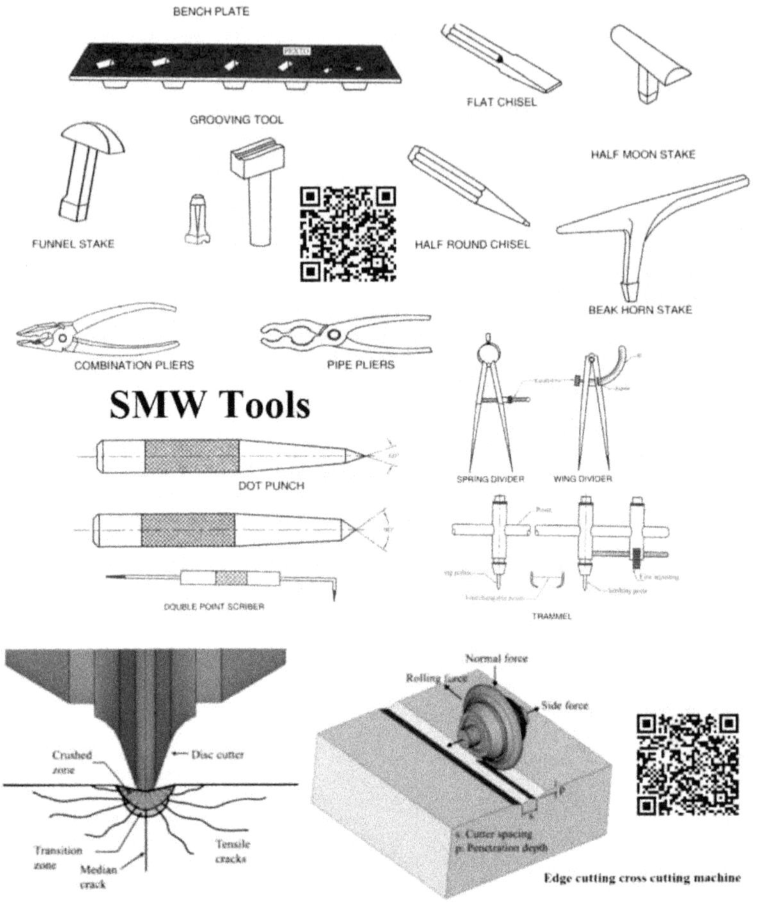
BENCH PLATE
FLAT CHISEL
GROOVING TOOL
HALF MOON STAKE
FUNNEL STAKE
HALF ROUND CHISEL
BEAK HORN STAKE
COMBINATION PLIERS
PIPE PLIERS
SMW Tools
DOT PUNCH
SPRING DIVIDER
WING DIVIDER
DOUBLE POINT SCRIBER
TRAMMEL
Normal force
Rolling force
Side force
Crushed zone
Disc cutter
Transition zone
Median crack
Tensile cracks
s: Cutter spacing
p: Penetration depth
Edge cutting cross cutting machine

CNC Press
Brake Machine

Plate Rolling Machine

Sheet Folding Machine

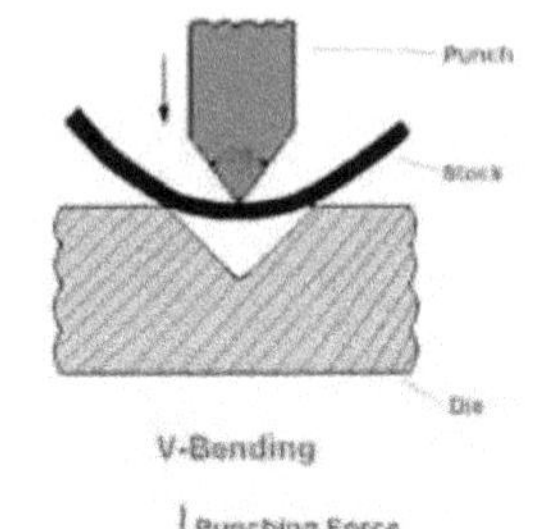

V-Bending

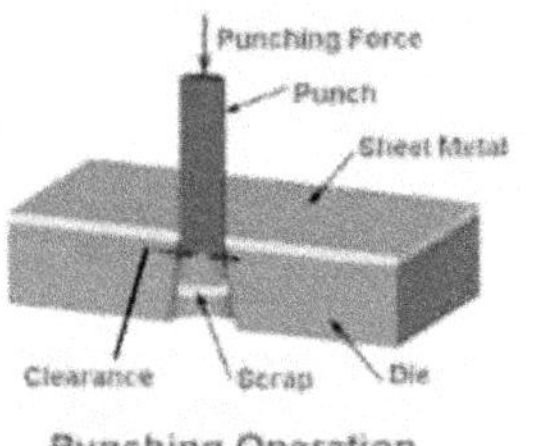

Punching Operation

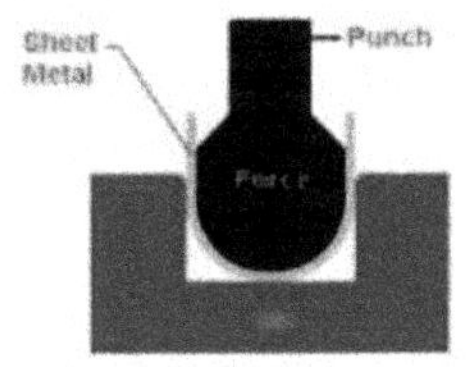

U-Bending

Hydraulic Shearing Machine

Rotary Shearing Machine

Pneumatic Shearing Machine

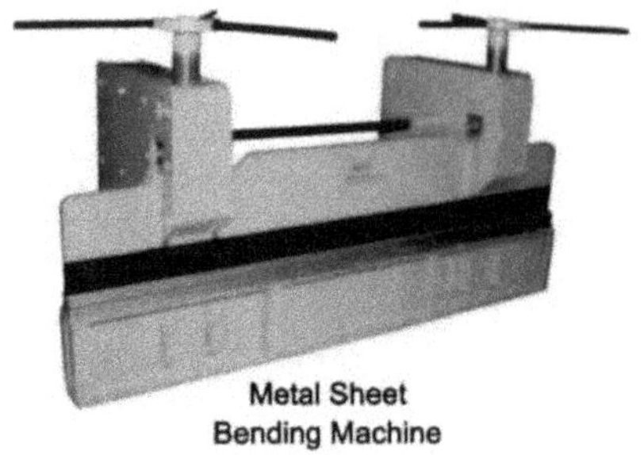
Metal Sheet
Bending Machine

Pipe Bending Machine

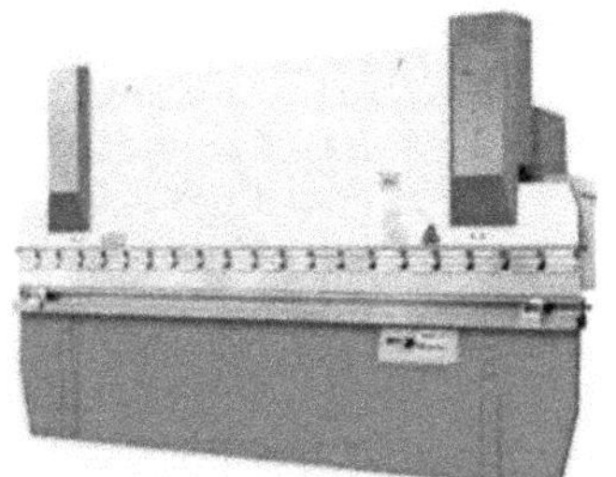
Hydraulic Press
Brake Machine

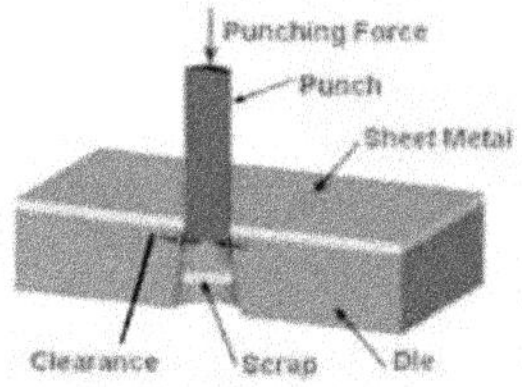

Punching Operation

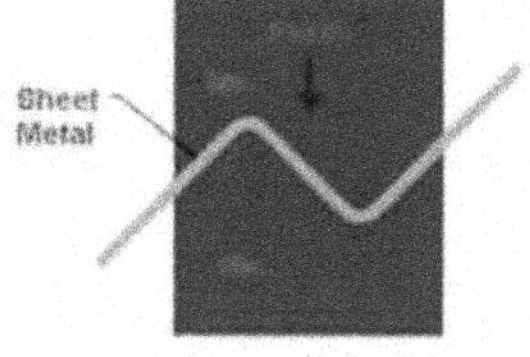

Offset Bending

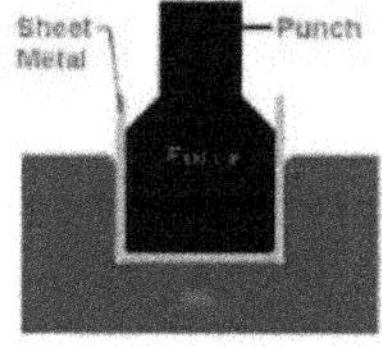

Channel Bending

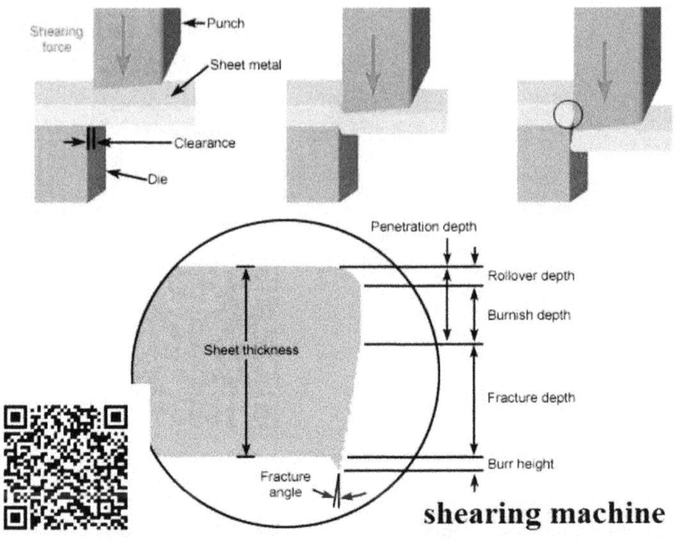

shearing machine

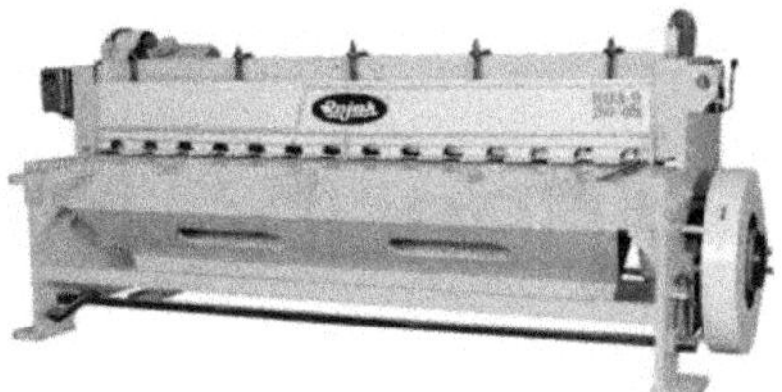

Mechanical Shearing Machine

Alligator Shearing Machine

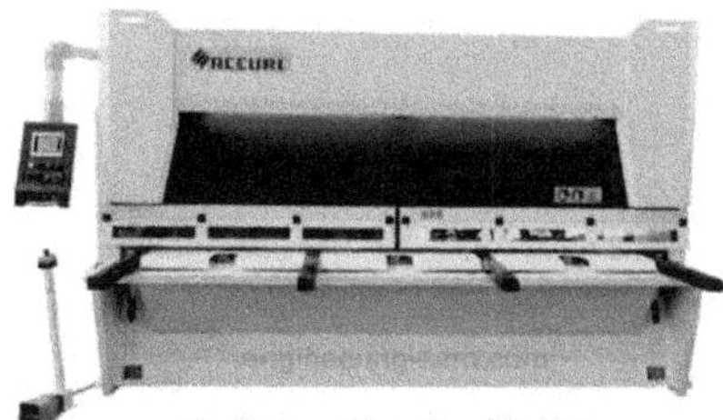

Guillotine Shearing Machine

CHAPTER EIGHT

Automobile Engineering MCQ

Automobile MCQ for Automobile Engineering

187] Fluid under pressures

A] To start heavy duty engine

B] Starter motor

C] Hydraulic cranking

D] Electric motor

188] Gasoline engine

A] To start heavy duty engine

B] Starter motor

C] Hydraulic cranking

D] Electric motor

189] Battery power

A] To start heavy duty engine

B] Starter motor

C] Hydraulic cranking

D] Electric motor

Starter winding armature in vehicle

190] Air compressor's driven by

A] To start heavy duty engine

B] Starter motor

C] Hydraulic cranking

D] Electric motor

191] Hydraulic floor jack is used

A] To remove king pin bush

B] To lift the wheel

C] To press the bush

D] Hold the job.

192] The most popular chuck on surface grinder is ----------

A] Pneumatic chuck

B] Hydraulic chuck

C] Magnetic chuck

D] Three law chuck

193] Which one of the following is the advantage of pneumatic system?

A] For low cost layout

B] For increasing the rate of production

C] For better working environment

D] All of these

194] Allows fluid both way in and out of cylinder

A] Piston

B] Push Rod
C] Primary cup
D] Check valve
195] Relieves excess pressure of air from the air tank.
A] Air compressor
B] Unloader valve
C] Safety valve
D] Brake chamber

Air tank safety valve

196] Regulates maximum air pressure, reaching to air tank.
A] Air compressor
B] Unloader valve
C] Safety valve
D] Brake chamber

Brakes in car

197] Supplies air to front and rear brake
A] Brake actuator
B] Dual brake valve
C] System protection valve
D] Flick valve
198] Operated for parking the vehicle.

A] Brake actuator
B] Dual brake valve
C] System protection valve
D] Flick valve
199] Distributes air to various circuits
A] Brake actuator
B] Dual brake valve
C] System protection valve
200] Keeps valves in closed position
A] Push Rod
B] Tappet
C] Spring
D] Cam lobe

Engine valves

201] Allow fuel to flow in and out
A] Valves
B] Coil spring

C] Diaphragm
D] Rocker arm

Cooling system in car

202] Allows coolants into the expansion tank
A] <u>Pressure relief valve</u>
B] Engine fan belt
C] Radiator drain plug
D] Over flow pipe
203] An overflow valve is used
A] <u>to send back excess fuel from the fuel filler</u>
B] to supply more fuel to the fuel filter
C] to supply clean fuel
D] to take the leaking fuel.
204] Provides compressed air to system
A] <u>Air compressor</u>
B] Unloader valve
C] Safety valve
D] Brake chamber

205] Air compressor's driven by
A] To start heavy duty engine
B] Starter motor
C] Hydraulic cranking
D] Electric motor
206] Air compressors is used for
A] Multipurpose
B] To lift the car only
C] To lift and remove the wheel
D] To grind the chisel.
207] in the air compressor, the safety device is used to
A] To suck the air
B] To release the air completely
C] To regulate the air pressure
D] To release excess air pressure.
208] Used in air compressor
A] Pressure gauge
B] Oil tank
C] Oil spray gun
D] Car hoist
209] Increases road wheel torque
A] Engine
B] Clutches
C] Final drive
D] U joints
210] Helps to turn the stub axles
A] Front axle
B] Track rod
C] Stub axle
D] Stub axle arm
211] Carries springs and steering linkages.
A] Front axle
B] Track rod
C] Stub axle
D] Stub axle arm

Steering gearbox in vehicle

212] Transmits steering wheel movement to stub axle

A] Front axle

B] Track rod

C] Stub axle

D] Stub axle arm

213] Pivots about king pin for steering purpose

A] Front axle

B] Track rod

C] Stub axle

D] Stub axle arm

214] Fuel catching fire

A] T.D.C.

B] Cycle

C] B.D.C.

D] Ignition

215] To seal the tank externally.

A] Baffles

B] Filter cap

C] Passage in the baffle

D] Filler neck

216] Prevents slashing of fuel in the tank

A] Baffles

B] Filter cap

C] Passage in the baffle

D] Filler neck

217] To fill fuel in the tank

A] Baffles
B] Filter cap
C] Passage in the baffle
D] Filler neck
218] To transfer fuel from one compartment to other compartment
A] Baffles
B] Filter cap
C] Passage in the baffle
D] Filler neck
219] Carries fuel
A] Carburettor
B] Pump
C] Pipe lines
D] Petrol tank
220] Stores petrol
A] Carburettor
B] Pump
C] Pipe lines
D] Petrol tank
221] Delivers petrol to the engine
A] Carburettor
B] Pump
C] Pipe lines
D] Petrol tank
222] Delivers petrol to carburettor
A] Carburettor
B] Pump
C] Pipe lines
D] Petrol tank

Fuel pump in Vehicle

223] Holds petrol
A] Air horn
B] Fuel bowl
C] Air cleaner
D] Air bleed
224] Serves as passage for air
A] Air horn
B] Fuel bowl
C] Air cleaner
D] Air bleed
225] Helps in breaking up fuel particles
A] Air horn
B] Fuel bowl
C] Air cleaner
D] Air bleed
226] Develops pressure on fuel to go out

A] Valves
B] Coil spring
C] Diaphragm
D] Rocker arm
227] Used to lift the vehicle
A] Pressure gauge
B] Oil tank
C] Oil spray gun
D] Car hoist
228] Used in car hoist
A] Pressure gauge
B] Oil tank
C] Oil spray gun
D] Car hoist
229] In diesel cycle Combustion takes place at
A] Constant pressure
B] Constant volume' '
C] Constant temperature
D] Constant temperature and pressure.
230] Rudolf Diesel, developed a Cl.engine
A] 1876
B] 1880
C] 1892
D] 1930

Engine in vehicle

231] Perkins built 'P' series engines
A] 1876
B] 1880
C] 1892
D] 1930
232] N.A OTTO developed a 4 stroke cycle engine
A] 1876
B] 1880
C] 1892
D] 1930
233] Dugald Clerk developed a 2 stroke cycle engine
A] 1876
B] 1880
C] 1892
D] 1930
234] All cylinders in a horizontal line
A] 'V' Engine
B] Inline Engine
C] Opposed Engine
D] Radial Engine
235] Cylinders positioned in 'V' shape
A] 'V' Engine

B] Inline Engine
C] Opposed Engine
D] Radial Engine
236] Cylinders positioned radially
A] 'V' Engine
B] Inline Engine
C] Opposed Engine
D] Radial Engine
237] Cylinders arranged horizontally opposite to each other
A] 'V' Engine
B] Inline Engine
C] Opposed Engine
D] Radial Engine
238] Indicate rate of battery charging current
A] Ammeter
B] Speedometer
C] Clutch pedal
D] Ignition switch
239] indicates the speed in Km/Hr
A] Ammeter
B] Speedometer
C] Clutch pedal
D] Ignition switch
240] Allow to flow the current in starting circuit in engine
A] Ammeter
B] Speedometer
C] Clutch pedal
D] Ignition switch
241] What IS the reason for hissing noise from cylinder head?
A] excessive tappet clearance
B] wrong injection timing
C] pie-ignition
D] air cleaner mounting loose.
242] Mounted on cylinder head or block
A] Fins
B] Radiators
C] Fan
D] Water pump

243] Which component among the following reduces noise of exhaust gases?

A] Exhaust pipe

B] Muffler

C] inlet manifold

D] tail pipe.

244] Specific gravity of battery electrolyte is checked by

A] ammeter

B] Voltmeter

C] Hydrometer

D] Tachometer.

Lead acid battery in vehicle

245] Oil level is checked by

A] Dip stick

B] Ammeter

C] Oil pressure gauge

D] Fuel gauge.

246] Used as parking light Cum indicator

A] A symmetrical bulb

B] Miniature bulb

C] Festoon bulb

D] S.C./ S.F.

247] Used as no plate lamp and brake lamp

B] Miniature bulb

C] Festoon bulb

D] S.C / S.F.

E] D.C/ D.F.

248] Used as two wheeler tail lamp
A] A symmetrical bulb
B] Miniature bulb
C] Festoon bulb
D] S.C/ S.F.
249] Used as panel instrument lamp
A] A symmetrical bulb
B] Miniature bulb
C] Festoon bulb
D] S.C.IS.F.
250] Used as headlight bulb
A] A symmetrical bulb
B] Miniature bulb
C] Festoon bulb
D] S.C.IS.F.
251] The head light parts can be replaced in
A] sealed beam
B] flush fitting type
C] prefocused bulb
D] halogen bulbs.
252] The head light is also used as
A] Side indicator
B] Stop indicator
C] Signalling device
D] Heating device.
253] To direct the shell light rays onto the road
A] Headlamp
B] Reflector
C] Lens
D] Adopter
254] To hold the bulb in the holder
A] Headlamp
B] Reflector
C] Lens
D] Adopter
255] To produce illumination
B] Reflector
C] Lens

D] Adopter
E] Bulb
256] To produce flat oval shaped beam
A] Headlamp
B] Reflector
C] Lens
D] Adopter
257] To hold the reflector in position
A] Headlamp
B] Reflector
C] Lens
D] Adopter
258] To indicate the vehicle is being braked
A] Headlight
B] Parking light
C] Stop light
D] Panel light
259] To read the working of gauges
A] Headlight
B] Parking light
C] Stop light
D] Panel light
260] To provide illumination on the road
A] Headlight
B] Parking light
C] Stop light
D] Panel light
261] to indicate the parking ' of vehicle
A] Headlight
B] Parking light
C] Stop light
D] Panel light
262] Feed pumps are driven by
A] camshaft of engine
B] Camshaft of FIP
C] Timing Gears
D] Varies from engine to engine.
263] The oil pumps are generally driven by

A] camshaft
B] rocker shaft
C] crankshaft
D] damper pulley
264]Engine develops less power due to
A]defective ignition timing
B]excessive rich mixture
C]defective lubrication system
D]too tight cylinder head
265] Supplies fluid to front and rear wheels
A] Brake pedal
B] Master cylinder piston
C] Wheel cylinder piston
D] Distribution block
266] Pushes the brake shoe towards drum
A] Brake pedal
B] Master cylinder piston
C] Wheel cylinder piston
D] Distribution block

Piston & rings in Engine

267] Creates pressure on fluid
A] Brake pedal
B] Master cylinder piston
C] Wheel cylinder piston
D] Distribution block

268] Pushes master cylinder piston through linkages.

A] Brake pedal

B] Master cylinder piston

C] Wheel cylinder piston

D] Distribution block

269] Allows fluid both way in and out of cylinder

A] Piston

B] Push Rod

C] Primary cup

D] Check valve

270] Seals the compensating port

A] Piston

B] Push Rod

C] Primary cup

D] Check valve

271] Actuates the piston

A] Piston

B] Push Rod

C] Primary cup

D] Check valve

272] Develops pressure on fluid

A] Piston

B] Push Rod

C] Primary cup

D] Check valve

273] Displacement volume of piston

A] |.H.P.

B] Swept volume

C] Mechanical efficiency

D] Horse power

274] Starting point of piston's downward movement in the cylinder

A] T.D.C.

B] Cycle

C] B.D.C.

D] Ignition

275] Starting point of piston's upward movement in the cylinder

A] T.D.C.

B] Cycle

C] B.D.C.
D] Ignition
276] Prevents blow by
A] Piston
B] Piston pin
C] Connecting rod
D] Piston rings
277] Reciprocates in the cylinder
A] Piston
B] Piston pin
C] Connecting rod
D] Piston rings
278] Connects piston and connecting rod
A] Piston
B] Piston pin
C] Connecting rod
D] Piston rings
279] Oscillates in cylinder
A] Piston
B] Piston pin
C] Connecting rod
D] Piston rings
280]The top and bottom halves of connecting rod are bolted on
A] crankshaft man journal
B] crankpin journal
C] camshaft
D] piston pin boss
281] A hole is drilled between crankshaft main journal and crank pin for
A] balancing of crankshaft
B] reducing crankshaft weight
C] lubricating connecting rod bearings
D] reducing crankshaft vibrations
282] Converts reciprocating motion into rotary motion
A] Crankshaft
B] Flywheels
C] Torque wrench
D] Thrust bearing
283] Rotary movement to pull and push action

A] Wiper motor
B] Cranking link
C] Pinion
D] Wiper blade
284] Accommodates wheel hub bearings.
A] Kingpin
B] Spring pad
C] Stub axle shaft portion
D] Track rod ball joints
285] Pushes with drawal plate
A] Clutch cover
B] Release bearing
C] Release fingers
D] Clutch plate
286] Takes thrust load
A] Crankshaft
B] Flywheels
C] Torque wrench
D] Thrust bearing
287]Distributor shaft is supported by
A] ball bearing
B] shell bearing
C] bush bearing
D] needle bearing
288] Stores energy
A] Crankshaft
B] Flywheels
C] Torque wrench
D] Thrust bearing
289] engages with the flywheel ring
A] Pinion
B] Over running clutch
C] Plunger disk
D] Clutch
290] Flywheel magneto consists of
A] Temporary magnet
B] Bar magnet
C] Permanent magnet

D] Needle magnet.

291] in flywheel magneto, the ignition coil is

A] stationary

B] Moving

C] Rotating

D] Oscillating.

292] To rotate the permanent magnet

A] Switch

B] Secondary coils

C] Flywheels

D] Condensers

293]The boiling temperature of the coolant in the cooling in the cooling system is increased by the use of

A]water jackets

B]vacuum valve only

C]pressure type radiator cap

D] radiator core tubes/pipes

Radiator cap in vehicle

294] The main purpose of pressure radiator cap is to

A]pressurize the system

B]increase air water circulation

C]help to develop vacuum in the system

D]avoid build up to pressure

295] one of the following causes may also contribute to overheating of an engine

A]clogged radiator cores

B]low idle speed setting

C]excessive valve tappet clearance

D]lubricating oil pressure is too high

296] Mounted on cylinder head or block

A] Fins

B] Radiators

C] Fan

D] Water pump

297] Drives the water pump

A] Pressure relief valve

B] Engine fan belt

C] Radiator drain plug

D] Over flow pipe

Thermostat valve in vehicle

298] If thermostat valve remains in an open position then which of the following will happen

A]slow warming up to engine

B]engine will over heat

C]engine fails to start

D]stalling of engine

299]In a dry sump lubrication system, a scavenging pump is used to

A] pump oil from sump to tank

B] pump oil directly to all moving parts

C] develop additional oil pressure

D] pump oil from tank to sum

300]Excessive oil pressure in the lubrication system may be due to

A] less quantity of engine oil in sump

B] incorrect adjustment of relief valve

C] less suction effect on the suction pipe

D] none of the above

301] when oil pressure increases above set limit, oil returns to sump through

A]pressure relief valve

B]by pass valve

C]oil filter

D]oil pump

302] low engine oil pressure may be due to

A]clogged oil filter

B]more oil filled in the oil sump

C]high viscosity of oil used

D]excessive backlash between pump gears

303] Cleans the air entering the cylinder

A] Air horn

B] Fuel bowl

C] Air cleaner

D] Air bleed

304] connect two terminals of solenoid.

A] Pinion

B] Over running clutch

C] Plunger disk

D] Clutch

305] When the horn button is pressed the current flows to horn through

A] Horn switch

B] Solenoid coil

C] Battery

D] Chassis.

306] Turns core to magnet

A] Solenoid Switch

B] Actuating wire (when heated]

C] Ballast Resistors

D] Actuating wire (when cooled]

307] What IS the reason for hissing noise from cylinder head?

A] excessive tappet clearance

B] wrong injection timing

C] pie-ignition

D] air cleaner mounting loose.

1] Disconnects engine for gear change

A] Engine

B] Clutches

C] Final drive

D] U joints

2] Pulls out pressure plate.

A] Clutch cover

B] Release bearing

C] Release fingers

D] Clutch plate

3] Transmits engine torque to transmission shaft.

A] Clutch cover

B] Release bearing

C] Release fingers

D] Clutch plate

4] Pushes with drawl plate

A] Clutch cover

B] Release bearing

C] Release fingers

D] Clutch plate

5] Holds pressure plate with fly wheel

A] Clutch cover

B] Release bearing

C] Release fingers

D] Clutch plate

6] Used in gear box

A] Multi plate clutch

B] Dog clutch

C] Cone clutch

D] Diaphragm clutch

Dog clutches in vehicle

7] provides more frictional area
A] Multi plate clutch
B] Dog clutch
C] Cone clutch
D] Diaphragm clutch
8] smaller flywheel is used
A] Multi plate clutch
B] Dog clutch
C] Cone clutch
D] Diaphragm clutch
9] Spring acts as a release lever
A] Multi plate clutch
B] Dog clutch
C] Cone clutch
D] Diaphragm clutch
10] Type of drive mechanism
A] Pinion
B] Over running clutch
C] Plunger disk
D] Clutch
11] Prevents over speeding of pinion and armature
A] Pinion
B] Over running clutch
C] Plunger disk
D] Clutch
12] Engages with the flywheel ring
A] Pinion

B] Over running clutch
C] Plunger disk
D] Clutch
13] Connect two terminals of solenoid.
A] Pinion
B] Over running clutch
C] Plunger disk
D] Clutch
14] Double declutch IS not necessary
A] Sliding mesh
B] Synchromesh
C] Double declutching
D] Transfer case
15] Used in four-wheel drive vehicle
A] Sliding mesh
B] Synchromesh
C] Double declutching
D] Transfer case
16] Only spur gears are used
A] Sliding mesh
B] Synchromesh
C] Double declutching
D] Transfer case
17] Used for smooth gear shifting
A] Sliding mesh
B] Synchromesh
C] Double declutching
D] Transfer case
18] Hard gear shifting is due to
A] Worn out clutch disc
B] Damaged main shaft bearings
C] Synchronizer unit damaged
D] excessive oil in the gearbox.

Gear

19] Gear slip is due to

A] Worn out synchroniser

B] Worn out clutch disc

C] Dry main shaft bearing

D] Weak pressure spring of clutch.

20] Noise in particular gear is due to

A] Insufficient clutch pedal free play

B] Damage gear teeth

C] Cracked gear box case

D] Damaged synchromesh unit.

21] While reversing the vehicle the driver should control

A] Clutch

B] Forward gear

C] Accelerator

D] Hand brake.

22] The clutch plate assembly has a centre steel disc riveted with springs for

A] strength

B] flexibility

C] less noise

D] absorbing shocks

23] Dog clutches are used in

A] gear boxes

B] friction clutches

C] brakes

D] differentials

Speed gear box in vehicle

24] Synchromesh mechanisms is provided for

A] Increasing the speed of the vehicle

B] Reducing the speed of the vehicle

C] Smooth gear engagement'

D] None of the above.

25] Only spur gears are used

A] Sliding mesh

B] Synchromesh

C] Double declutching

D] Transfer case

26] Used for smooth gear shifting

A] Sliding mesh

B] Synchromesh

C] Double declutching

D] Transfer case

27] Hard gear shifting is due to

A] Worn out clutch disc

B] Damaged main shaft bearings

C] Synchronizer unit damaged

D] Excessive oil in the gearbox.

28] Gear slip is due to

A] Worn out synchroniser

B] Worn out clutch disc

C] Dry main shaft bearing

D] Weak pressure spring of clutch.

29] Noise in particular gear is due to

A] Insufficient clutch pedal free play

B] Damage gear teeth

C] Cracked gear box case

D] Damaged synchromesh unit.

30] Gearshift lever is used for

A] Releasing clutch

B] Changing gear

C] Increasing the speed of the engine

D] Controlling the direction of vehicle.

31] In which type of steering gear box variable steering ration is achieved?

A] worm and roller steering gear

B] worm and nut steering gear

C] worm and sector steering gear

D] rack and pinion steering gear

Steering gearbox in vehicle

32] The vehicle attains different speed by means of

A] gear box

B] clutch

C] differential

D] rear axle & wheel

33] Dog clutches are used in

A] gear boxes

B] friction clutches

C] brakes

D] differentials

34] in a 3 speed gear box in following combination of gears are provided

A] 3 forward and 1 reverse

B] 2 forward and 1 reverse

C] 4 forward

D] 2 forward and 2 reverse

35] which gear does not produce axial trust

A] spur gear

B] helical gear

C] spiral bevel gear

D] bevel gear

36] which gears converts rotary motion into linear motion

A] worm gears

B] herring bone gear

C] rack & pinion

D] helical gear

37] What is a reason for gear slip

A] unlubricated gear linka-ges

B] less oil in gear box

C] broken teeth of gear

D] wrong adjustment of gear lever

38] In a differential gear ratio can be calculated from any one of the following statements

A] sun gear

B] planetary gear

C] crown wheel

D] pinion

Differential gear box in truck

39] low engine oil pressure may be due to

A] clogged oil filter

B] more oil filled in the oil sump

C] high viscosity of oil used

D] excessive backlash between pump gears

40] Increases road wheel torque

A] Engine

B] Clutches

C] Final drive

D] U joints

41] Used in four-wheel drive vehicle

A] Sliding mesh

B] Synchromesh

C] Double declutching

D] Transfer case

42] Four wheel drive should be used

A] Always

B] While climbing up hill

C] On sand (slushy ground)
D] While climbing down hill.
43] While driving in a wet or sandy roads always use
A] Four wheel drive only
B] Two wheel drive only
C] First gear only
D] More acceleration.
44] Fluid under pressures
A] To start heavy duty engine
B] Starter motor
C] Hydraulic cranking
D] Electric motor
45] Gasoline engine
A] To start heavy duty engine
B] Starter motor
C] Hydraulic cranking
D] Electric motor
46] Battery power
A] To start heavy duty engine
B] Starter motor
C] Hydraulic cranking
D] Electric motor
47] Air compressor's driven by
A] To start heavy duty engine
B] Starter motor
C] Hydraulic cranking
D] Electric motor
48] Hydraulic floor jack is used
A] To remove king pin bush
B] To lift the wheel
C] To press the bush
D] Hold the job.
49]The pressure of fluid in hydraulic brake system is governed by
A] boils law
B] Charles law
C] Pascal's law
D] none of the above laws
50] the fluid pressure in master cylinder depends on

A] master cylinder piston area
B] wheel cylinder piston area
C] pipe line dia
D] fluid viscosity
51] Allows fluid both way in and out of cylinder
A] Piston
B] Push Rod
C] Primary cup
D] Check valve
52] Seals the compensating port
A] Piston
B] Push Rod
C] Primary cup
D] Check valve
53] Actuates the piston
A] Piston
B] Push Rod
C] Primary cup
D] Check valve
54] Develops pressure on fluid
A] Piston
B] Push Rod
C] Primary cup
D] Check valve

Piston & rings in Engine

55] Develops pressure on fuel to go out

A] Valves

B] Coil spring

C] Diaphragm

D] Rocker arm

56] Actuates the diaphragm

A] Valves

B] Coil spring

C] Diaphragm

D] Rocker arm

57] Allow fuel to flow in and out

A] Valves

B] Coil spring

C] Diaphragm

D] Rocker arm

Engine valves

58] Helps to return the diaphragm.

A] Valves
B] Coil spring
C] Diaphragm
D] Rocker arm
59] An overflow valve is used
A] to send back excess fuel from the fuel filler
B] to supply more fuel to the fuel filter
C] to supply clean fuel
D] to take the leaking fuel.
60] Excessive oil pressure in the lubrication system may be due to
A] less quantity of engine oil in sump
B] incorrect adjustment of relief valve
C] less suction effect on the suction pipe
D] none of the above
61] when oil pressure increases above set limit, oil returns to sump through
A] pressure relief valve
B] by pass valve
C] oil filter
D] oil pump
62] Helps to turn the stub axles
A] Front axle
B] Track rod
C] Stub axle
D] Stub axle arm
63] Carries springs and steering linkages.
A] Front axle
B] Track rod
C] Stub axle
D] Stub axle arm
64] Transmits steering wheel movement to stub axle
A] Front axle
B] Track rod
C] Stub axle
D] Stub axle arm
65] Pivots about king pin for steering purpose
A] Front axle
B] Track rod

C] Stub axle
D] Stub axle arm
66] Acts as a seat for spring mounting
A] Kingpin
B] Spring pad
C] Stub axle shaft portion
D] Track rod ball joints
67] Connects front axle with stub axle
A] Kingpin
B] Spring pad
C] Stub axle shaft portion
D] Track rod ball joints
68] Provides flexible movement for track rod
A] Kingpin
B] Spring pad
C] Stub axle shaft portion
D] Track rod ball joints
69] Accommodates wheel hub bearings.
A] Kingpin
B] Spring pad
C] Stub axle shaft portion
D] Track rod ball joints
70] Pivots on the bottom of frame and acts as a seat for spring
A] Upper control arm
B] Coil spring
C] Ball joints
D] Lower control arm
71] Acts as pivot for steering knuckle movement
A] Upper control arm
B] Coil spring
C] Ball joints
D] Lower control arm
72] Provides cushioning effect
A] Upper control arm
B] Coil spring
C] Ball joints
D] Lower control arm
73] Pivots on the top of frame and acts as a seat for spring

A] Upper control arm
B] Coil spring
C] Ball joints
D] Lower control arm

74] When front wheels are in straight ahead position and lines are drawn through king pins centre and steering arms end, at which point they will meet?
A] At centre of front axle
B] At centre of chassis
C] At centre of rear axle behind differential
D] At centre of rear axle just ahead of differential

75] Transmits its motion to meshing parts
A] Steering wheel
B] Worm
C] Steering column
D] Sector/roller/ball nut/peg

76] Rotates the steering column
A] Steering wheel
B] Worm
C] Steering column
D] Sector/roller/ball nut/peg

77] Rotates in an arc movement and transmits it to cross shaft
A] Steering wheel
B] Worm
C] Steering column
D] Sector/roller/ball nut/peg

78] Rotates the worm
A] Steering wheel
B] Worm
C] Steering column
D] Sector/roller/ball

79] Outward tilt of front wheel
A] Negative camber angle
B] Positive caster angle
C] Kingpin inclination
D] Included angle vehicle

80] Inward tilt of front wheel
A] Negative camber angle

B] Positive caster angle

C] Kingpin inclination

D] Included angle vehicle

81] The angle between tyre centre line and kingpin centre line

A] Negative camber angle

B] Positive caster angle

C] Kingpin inclination

D] Included angle vehicle

82] Tilt of kingpin towards centre of vehicle

A] Negative camber angle

B] Positive caster angle

C] Kingpin inclination

D] Included angle vehicle

83] In which type of steering gear box variable steering ration is achieved?

A] worm and roller steering gear

B] worm and nut steering gear

C] worm and sector steering gear

D] rack and pinion steering gear

84] A strut rod in a suspension is used in

A] conventional I beam axle type suspension

B] coil spring type suspension system

C] torsion bar suspension system

D] Macpherson system

85] Carries springs and steering linkages.

A] Front axle

B] Track rod

C] Stub axle

D] Stub axle arm

86] Acts as a seat for spring mounting

A] Kingpin

B] Spring pad

C] Stub axle shaft portion

D] Track rod ball joints

87] Pivots on the bottom of frame and acts as a seat for spring

A] Upper control arm

B] Coil spring

C] Ball joints

D] Lower control arm

88] Provides cushioning effect

A] Upper control arm

B] Coil spring

C] Ball joints

D] Lower control arm

89] in a Hotchkiss drive rear and driving torque is taken up by

A] rear axle housing

B] rear leaf spring

C] shock absorber

D] engine mountings

90] Helper spring is used in

A] Cars

B] jeep

C] light motor vehicle

D] heavy trucks

91] The angle between tyre centre line and kingpin centre line

A] Negative camber angle

B] Positive caster angle

C] Kingpin inclination

D] Included angle vehicle

92] Bald spots appearing on tyre's outer surface is due to

A] Excessive speed

B] lack of rotation of tyres

C] unbalanced wheel

D] over inflation

93] The angle between centre line of king pin and a vertical line from centre point of tyre is called

A. camber angle

B. caster angle

C. toe out angle on turns

D. kingpin inclination

94] Brings back the pedal to normal position

A] Brake pedal

B] Linkage

C] Cam

D] Pedal return spring

95] Expands the brake shoe

A] Brake pedal
B] Linkage
C] Cam
D] Pedal return spring
96] Operates the cam
A] Brake pedal
B] Linkage
C] Cam
D] Pedal return spring
97] Operates the linkages
A] Brake pedal
B] Linkage
C] Cam
D] Pedal return spring
98] Supplies fluid to front and rear wheels
A] Brake pedal
B] Master cylinder piston
C] Wheel cylinder piston
D] Distribution block
99] Pushes the brake shoe towards drum
A] Brake pedal
B] Master cylinder piston
C] Wheel cylinder piston
D] Distribution block
100] Creates pressure on fluid
A] Brake pedal
B] Master cylinder piston
C] Wheel cylinder piston
D] Distribution block
101] Pushes master cylinder piston through linkages.
A] Brake pedal
B] Master cylinder piston
C] Wheel cylinder piston
D] Distribution block
102] Allows fluid both way in and out of cylinder
A] Piston
B] Push Rod
C] Primary cup

D] Check valve

103] Seals the compensating port

A] Piston

B] Push Rod

C] Primary cup

D] Check valve

104] Actuates the piston

A] Piston

B] Push Rod

C] Primary cup

D] Check valve

105] Develops pressure on fluid

A] Piston

B] Push Rod

C] Primary cup

D] Check valve

106] Among the following which material is not used for brake drum.

A] Steel

B] Copper

C] Cast iron

D] Aluminium alloy

107] The purpose of using a rubber boot at the ends of a wheel cylinder is...

A] to prevent entry of foreign particles

B] to allow air inside the cylinder

C] to allow return brake fluid to leak out

D] to stop exit of air from the cylinder

108] To reduce noise during reverse braking

A] Double piston wheel cylinder

B] Single piston wheel cylinder

C] Step-bore wheel cylinder

D] Baffle type wheel cylinders

109] To increase braking force on shoes

A] Double piston wheel cylinder

B] Single piston wheel cylinder

C] Step-bore wheel cylinder

D] Baffle type wheel cylinders

110] For operating two leading shoe brakes

A] Double piston wheel cylinder
B] Single piston wheel cylinder
C] Step-bore wheel cylinder
D] Baffle type wheel cylinders
111] For operating leading and trailing shoe brakes
A] Double piston wheel cylinder
B] Single piston wheel cylinder
C] Step-bore wheel cylinder
D] Baffle type wheel cylinders

Air tank safety valve

112] Relieves excess pressure of air from the air tank.
A] Air compressor
B] Unloader valve
C] Safety valve
D] Brake chamber

Brakes in car

113] Houses diaphragm and pushrod
A] Air compressor

B] Unloader valve

C] Safety valve

D] <u>Brake chamber</u>

114] Provides compressed air to system

A] <u>Air compressor</u>

B] Unloader valve

C] Safety valve

D] Brake chamber

115] Regulates maximum air pressure, reaching to air tank.

A] Air compressor

B] <u>Unloader valve</u>

C] Safety valve

D] Brake chamber

116] How brakes are applied in fail safe brake system during parking

A] by air pressure in brake actuator

B] <u>By spring pressure in brake actuator</u>

C] by vacuum in brake actuator

D] by mechanical hand brake

117] Supplies air to front and rear brake

A] Brake actuator

B] <u>Dual brake valve</u>

C] System protection valve

D] Flick valve

118] Operated for parking the vehicle.

A] Brake actuator

B] Dual brake valve

C] System protection valve

D] <u>Flick valve</u>

119] Exerts spring pressure and applies brake when air pressure in system is less

A] <u>Brake actuator</u>

B] Dual brake valve

C] System protection valve

D] Flick valve

120] Distributes air to various circuits

A] Brake actuator

B] Dual brake valve

C] <u>System protection valve</u>

D] Flick valve

121] To indicate the vehicle is being braked

A] Headlight

B] Parking light

C] Stop light

122] Used as no plate lamp and brake lamp

B] Miniature bulb

C] Festoon bulb

D] S.C / S.F.

E] D.C/ D.F.

123] parkingbreakes are generally operated by

A] hand lever operation

B] brake pedal operation

C] electrical switch control operation

D] none of the above

124]The pressure of fluid in hydraulic brake system is governed by

A] boils law

B] Charles law

C] Pascal's law

D] none of the above laws

125] The fluid pressure in master cylinder depends on

A] master cylinder piston area

B] wheel cylinder piston area

C] pipe line dia

D] fluid viscosity

126] the tandem master has

A] two reservoirs and two outlets

B] one reservoir and two outlets

C] tow reservoir and one outlet

D] one reservoir and one outlet

127] Which defects of brake drum cannot be corrected by turning?

A] taper

B] over heating

C] ovality

D] scoring

128]The fluid pressure in a wheel cylinder can be increased by any one of the following methods

A] by changing dia of piston

B] by changing dia of rubber cup
C] by changing the spring
D] by interchanging of brake shoes
129] Air tank is made of
A]steel
B] copper
C] plastic
D] brass
130] Safety valve on air tank prevents
A] oil accumulation in air tank
B] excess air reaching to brake valve
C] bursting of air tank at high pressure
D] vehicle to move when brake has failed
131] How many air tanks are used in dual air brake system
A] one
B] two
C] three
D] four
132] Person acts as a steerman of the vehicle is called
A] conductor
B] Driver
C] Passenger
D] spectator.
133] Act for leaving the vehicle in dangerous position
A] 125 of MV ACT 1988
B] 126 of MV ACT 1988
C] 128 of MV ACT 1988
D] 122 of MV ACT 1988
134] Act for Riding on running board
B] 126 of MV ACT 1988
C] 128 of MV ACT 1988
D] 122 of MV ACT 1988
E] 123 of MV ACT 1988
135] Act for Obstruction of driver
A] 125 of MV ACT 1988
B] 126 of MV ACT 1988
C] 128 of MV ACT 1988
D] 122 of MV ACT 1988

136] Act for Stationary vehicles
A] 125 of MV ACT 1988
B] 126 of MV ACT 1988
C] 128 of MV ACT 1988
D] 122 of MV ACT 1988
137] Act for Safety measures for drivers and pillion riders
A] 125 of MV ACT 1988
B] 126 of MV ACT 1988
C] 128 of MV ACT 1988
D] 122 of MV ACT 1988
138] Carries fuel
A] Carburettor
B] Pump
C] Pipe lines
D] Petrol tank
139] Stores petrol
A] Carburettor
B] Pump
C] Pipe lines
D] Petrol tank
140] Delivers petrol to the engine
A] Carburettor
B] Pump
C] Pipe lines
D] Petrol tank
141] Delivers petrol to carburettor
A] Carburettor
B] Pump
C] Pipe lines
D] Petrol tank
142] Holds petrol
A] Air horn
B] Fuel bowl
C] Air cleaner
D] Air bleed
143] if petrol air mixture is compressed in a cylinder
A] its volume reduces
B] its pressure will rise

C] its temperature will increase

D] all the above will happen

144]During suction stroke the charge drawn in a petrol engine is

A] air only

B. air and petrol mixture

C] petrol only

D] fuels other than petrol

Petrol engine in car

145] In a petrol engine air fuel mixture is drawn into the cylinder due to vacuum created during

A] power stroke

B] exhaust stroke

C] suction stroke

D] compression stroke

146] the high fuel consumption of a petrol engine may be due to

A] leakage of fuel from carburetor

B] defects in lubrication system

C] air leaks in intake manifold

D] incorrect idle speed (too low)

147] the float circuit is provided in a carburetor

A] to store fuel vapours

B] to supply mixture of air & fuel

C] to maintain proper level of fuel in float chamber

D] none of the above

148] increase or decrease the speed of the engine

B] Speedometer

C] Clutch pedal

D] Ignition switch

E] Accelerator

Engine in vehicle

149] While allowing other vehicle to overtake

A] Accelerate

B] Reduce accelerator

C] Stop the vehicle

D] Move the vehicle to right.

150] Fuel catching fire

A] T.D.C.
B] Cycle
C] B.D.C.
D] Ignition
151] To seal the tank externally.
A] Baffles
B] Filter cap
C] Passage in the baffle
D] Filler neck
152] Prevents slashing of fuel in the tank
A] Baffles
B] Filter cap
C] Passage in the baffle
D] Filler neck
153] To fill fuel in the tank
A] Baffles
B] Filter cap
C] Passage in the baffle
D] Filler neck
154] To transfer fuel from one compartment to other compartment
A] Baffles
B] Filter cap
C] Passage in the baffle
D] Filler neck
155] Carries fuel
A] Carburettor
B] Pump
C] Pipe lines
D] Petrol tank
156] Stores petrol
A] Carburettor
B] Pump
C] Pipe lines
D] Petrol tank
157] Delivers diesel to the engine
A] Carburettor
B] Pump
C] Pipe lines

D] Petrol tank

158] Delivers diesel to carburettor

A] Carburettor

B] <u>Pump</u>

C] Pipe lines

D] Petrol tank

Fuel pump in Vehicle

159] Holds diesel

A] Air horn

B] <u>Fuel bowl</u>

C] Air cleaner

D] Air bleed

160] Serves as passage for air

A] <u>Air horn</u>

B] Fuel bowl

C] Air cleaner

D] Air bleed

161] Helps in breaking up fuel particles
A] Air horn
B] Fuel bowl
C] Air cleaner
D] Air bleed
162] Cleans the air entering the cylinder
A] Air horn
B] Fuel bowl
C] Air cleaner
D] Air bleed
163] Develops pressure on fuel to go out
A] Valves
B] Coil spring
C] Diaphragm
D] Rocker arm
164] Actuates the diaphragm
A] Valves
B] Coil spring
C] Diaphragm
D] Rocker arm
165] Allow fuel to flow in and out
A] Valves
B] Coil spring
C] Diaphragm
D] Rocker arm
166] When the engine temperature is high, the resistance in the engine unit becomes
A] less
B] More
C] remains constant
D] Fluctuates.
167] The actuating wire is made of
A] lead
B] Aluminium
C] Copper
D] nichrome
168] When the iron core turns to magnet it attracts
A] Main armature

B] Auxiliary armature
C] Both the armature
D] No armature.
169] Flasher unit terminals are marked as
A] HBS
B] LBP
C] ISB
D] ABF
170] Separates the points
A] Solenoid Switch
B] Actuating wire (when heated)
C] Ballast Resistors
D] Actuating wire (when cooled)
171] Limits the current to the points
A] Solenoid Switch
B] Actuating wire (when heated)
C] Ballast Resistors
D] Actuating wire (when cooled)
172] Closes the points
A] Solenoid Switch
B] Actuating wire (when heated)
C] Ballast Resistors
D] Actuating wire (when cooled)
173] Turns core to magnet
A] Solenoid Switch
B] Actuating wire (when heated)
C] Ballast Resistors
D] Actuating wire (when cooled)
174] Flywheel magneto consists of
A] Temporary magnet
B] Bar magnet
C] Permanent magnet
D] Needle magnet.
175] in flywheel magneto, the ignition coil is
A] stationary
B] Moving
C] Rotating
D] Oscillating.

176] To prevent arcing in the points
A] Switch
B] Secondary coils
C] Flywheels
D] Condensers
177] To complete primary circuit
A] Switch
B] Secondary coils
C] Flywheels
D] Condensers
178] To induce H.T. current
A] Switch
B] Secondary coils
C] Flywheels
D] Condensers
179] To rotate the permanent magnet
A] Switch
B] Secondary coils
C] Flywheels
D] Condensers
180] When the engine rotates the current is first produced in the
A] Secondary winding
B] Primary winding
C] Both the coil
D] Condenser
181] The C.B. points open due to rotation of
A] armature
B] Cam
C] Flywheel
D] Magnet.
182] Stores current and reverses the same
A] Armature
B] Spark plug
C] Condenser
D] Horse shoe
183] Produces magnetic field
A] Armature
B] Spark plug

C] Condenser
D] Horse shoe
184] Opens the contact breaker points
B] Spark plug
C] Condenser
D] Horse shoe
E] Cam
185] Rotates between magnetic poles
A] Armature
B] Spark plug
C] Condenser
D] Horse shoe
186] Converts H.T. current to spark.
A] Armature
B] Spark plug
C] Condenser
D] Horse shoe
187] The alternators are used in the vehicles to
A] Charge the battery
B] Measure current
C] Measure voltage
D] Discharge battery.

Dynamo (Alternator) distributor cap in car

188] The A.C. current of alternator win be converted to D.C by using

A] condenser

B] Rectifier

C] Brushes

D] Induction coil.

189] The carbon brushes ride on the

A] Commutator

B] Armature

C] Slip ring

D] Rotor.

190] The ends of stator winding attached to the

A] Field coil

B] Carbon brush

C] Copper brush

D] Diodes.

191] Consists no of coils in slot

A] Diode
B] Stator
C] Fingers
D] Heat sink
192] Forms 'S'& N poles
A] Diode
B] Stator
C] Fingers
D] Heat sink
193] Reads charging rate
B] Stator
C] Fingers
D] Heat sink
E] Ammeter
194] Absorbs the heat in diodes
A] Diode
B] Stator
C] Fingers
D] Heat sink
195] Made of silicon
A] Diode
B] Stator
C] Fingers
D] Heat sink
196] While fitting battery observe correct
A] Polarity
B] Mounting
C] Distilled water
D] Nothing
197] The output of the alternator is checked by
A] Flashing the leads
B] Looking
C] Using Instruments
D] Removing leads
198] Measures cell voltage
A] Resistance
B] Voltmeter
C] Ammeter

D] Cell tester

Lead acid battery in vehicle

199] Measures voltage of battery

A] Resistance

B] Voltmeter

C] Ammeter

D] Cell tester

200] Ohms is unit for

A] Resistance

B] Voltmeter

C] Ammeter

D] Cell tester

201] Fitted on panel board

A] Resistance

B] Voltmeter

C] Ammeter

D] Cell tester

202] If the thin cables are used for starter motor

A] Cable wilt get heated up

B] Voltage drop

C] Supply lesser current

D] Supply more current.

Starter winding armature in vehicle

203] The main feed wires from the battery consists the main colour of

A] White

B] Brown.

D] red

D] Black

204] Earth circuit colour

C] Blue/red

D] Red

E] Black

F] White

205] Front parking lamp colour

A] Brown

B] Yellow

C] Blue/red

D] Red

206] ignition circuit colour

C] Blue/red

D] Red

E] Black

F] White

207] Generating circuit colour

A] Brown

B] Yellow
C] Blue/red
D] Red
208] Head light circuit colour
A] Brown
B] Yellow
C] Blue/red
D] Red
209] Battery feed circuit colour
A] Brown
B] Yellow
C] Blue/red
D] Red
210] The movement of the slide arm of the tank unit changes as per
A] current
B] Speed
C] Fuel level
D] Oil level.
211] When the float rises above due to full tank than the resistance of the tank unit
A] Fluctuates
B] remains constant
C] Lowers.
D] Raises.
212] When the tank begins to empty the tank unit fioat
A] Falls down
B] Raise up
C] Vibrates
D] remains steady.
213] connect two terminals of solenoid.
A] Pinion
B] Over running clutch
C] Plunger disk
D] Clutch
214] The lamp switches are fitted on
A] Steering column
B] Panel board
C] Gearlever

D] Hand brake lever.
215] The lamps are protected from overloading by
A] Switch
B] Fuse
C] Holder
D] Harness
216] Used as two wheeler tail lamp
A] A symmetrical bulb
B] Miniature bulb
C] Festoon bulb
D] S.C/ S.F.
217] Used as panel instrument lamp
A] A symmetrical bulb
B] Miniature bulb
C] Festoon bulb
D] S.C.IS.F.
218] To hold the reflector in position
A] Headlamp
B] Reflector
C] Lens
D] Adopter
219] Front parking lamp colour
A] Brown
B] Yellow
C] Blue/red
D] Red
220] The bulb filament is in the form of
A] Spiral
B] Straight
C] Loop
D] Star.
221] Used as headlight bulb
A] A symmetrical bulb
B] Miniature bulb
C] Festoon bulb
D] S.C.IS.F.
222] The head light parts can be replaced in
A] Sealed beam

B] Flush fitting type
C] refocused bulb
D] Halogen bulbs.
223] The head light is also used as
A] Side indicator
B] Stop indicator
C] Signalling device
D] Heating device.
224] To direct the shell light rays onto the road
A] Headlamp
B] Reflector
C] Lens
D] Adopter
225] To hold the bulb in the holder
A] Headlamp
B] Reflector
C] Lens
D] Adopter
226] To produce illumination
B] Reflector
C] Lens
D] Adopter
E] Bulb
227] To produce flat oval shaped beam
A] Headlamp
B] Reflector
C] Lens
D] Adopter
228] To hold the reflector in position
A] Headlamp
B] Reflector
C] Lens
D] Adopter
229] When the horn button is pressed the current flows to the horn from the....
A] dynamo
B] battery
C] starter

D] Horn button.
230] Horn sound waves are produced due to
A] Arcing in horn points
B] Vibration of diaphragm
C] Closing of points
D] Opening of points.
231] Horn relay consists terminals of
A] IBC
B] BPL
C] ABF
D] HBS
232] To make and break the horn circuit
A] Horn relay
B] Horn switch
C] Horn points
D] Solenoid
233] To operate the relay
A] Horn relay
B] Horn switch
C] Horn points
D] Solenoid
234] To increase the horn frequency
B] Horn switch
C] Horn points
D] Solenoid
E] Tone disc
235] To supply maximum current from the battery to the horn
A] Horn relay
B] Horn switch
C] Horn points
D] Solenoid
236] When the horn button is pressed the current flows to horn through
A] Horn switch
B] Solenoid coil
C] Battery
D] Chassis.
237] When the horn button is pressed the button touches the
A] Grounded plate

B] Live plate
C] Both
D] None of these.
238] Horn sound can be corrected by
A] Higher capacity battery
B] Adjusting screw
B] Use more no. horn
D] Using thick fuse.
239] Horn sound become poor due to
A] Sticky point
B] Discharged battery
C] Charged battery
D] Blown fuse.
240] Serves as passage for air
A] Air horn
B] Fuel bowl
C] Air cleaner
D] Air bleed
241] The wiper motor receives current from the
A] dynamo
B] Starter motor
C] cut-out
D] Battery.
242] The type of wiper unit used in present day vehicles is
A] Electrical type
B] Hydraulic
C] Vacuum
D] mechanical.
243] The wiper blades mating faces are made of
A] Leather
B] Fabric
C] Rubber
D] Fibre
244] Rotary movement to pull and push action
A] Wiper motor
B] Cranking link
C] Pinion
D] Wiper blade

245] Operates arm and blade
A] Wiper motor
B] Cranking link
C] Pinion
D] Wiper blade
246] Converts electrical energy into mechanical energy
A] Wiper motor
B] Cranking link
C] Pinion
D] Wiper blade
247] Causes oscillation of blade
B] Cranking link
C] Pinion
D] Wiper blade
E] Cable
248] Clears water layer from the glass
A] Wiper motor
B] Cranking link
C] Pinion
D] Wiper blade

Safety Precaution for Automobile Engineering

01] In case of bleeding, take treatment Of
A] spray cold water
B] Bandage immediately -----]
C] Enquire about the accident thought treatment
D] cold 3" and rest
02] in case of an accident, the victim should im
A] Asked to take rest
C] Attended immediately
D] leave him
03] First aid is given to an injured or ill person primarily....
A] Save life
B] Prevent further deterioration of the muff's
C] Give best possible comfort
D] All of these
04] Colour code for Bins for waste paper segregation is -----
A] blue Colour
B] Yellow Colour

C] Red Colour

D] Green Colour

05] In Japanese Seiko stands for -------------

A] Shine

B] Sort

C] Standardize

D] Sustain

06] Benefit of SS system is ------

A] Increase in productivity

B] Increase in quality

C] Reduction in wastage of time

D] All of these

07] Safety is -----------

A] nobody's business

B] every bodise business

C] Some bodies business

D] The organization business

08] For basic categories of safety signs are available The meaning of"prohibition" sign ----

A] shows it must not be done

B] Shows what must be done

C] Warns the hazard or danger

D] Gives information of safety provision

09] Which one is a workshop safety?

A] Keep shop floor clean and free from grease, oil or other slippery materials

B] Stop the machine before changing the speed

C] Don't use cracked or chipped tools

D] Don't try to stop a running machine with hand

10] In Personal Protect Equipment (PPE] HELMET is used to

A] protect head

B] Protect eyes

C] Protect hands

D] Protect ears

11] Which of the following belongs to general safety?

A Have a worker in good attitude

B] The work clean and clear

C] Concentrate on your work

D] Keep the floor and gangways clean and clear

12] While grinding, which is used to protect the eyes?

A] Dark green glass

B] Mask

C] Sun glasses

D] Safety goggles

13] Which of the following is done for machine safety?

A] Check the oil level before starting the machine

B] Do things in a methodical way

C] Keep the floor and gangways clean and clear

D] Don't use dies and scarves

14] In Personal Protect Equipment (PPE], 'sleeves' is used to protect ----------

A] Face

B] Eyes

C] Ears

D] Hands

15] ABC stands for --------------

A] Automatic Breathing Control

B] Automatic Blood Control

C] Airway Breathing Circulation

D] Automatic Blood Circulation

16] To put off"Class B" fire, the types of fire extinguisher used is ....]

A] dry power

B] Carbon dioxide

C] Jet of water

D] Foam type

17] Which type of fire extinguisher is used to put off general fire?

A] Water type Extinguisher

B] Foam type Extinguisher

C] Dry chemical powder Extinguisher

D] Carbon dioxide (C02] Extinguisher

Hand Tools in Automobile Engineering

18] One micrometer (U] is equal to...

A] 0.1mm

B] 0.01mm

C] 0.001mm

D] 0.0001mm

19] Name the tool used to make and finish the leak proof joints of a pipe T joint

A] groover

B] setting hammer

C] creasing hammer

D] round bottom stake

20] Portion of the hammer used for fixing the handle is...

A] Face

B] Peen

C] Cheek

D] Eye hole

21] Weight of the hammer for the marking purpose is...

A] 250g

B] 500g

C] 1 kg

D] 2 kgs

22] To cut out small apertures which punch and die type of machine is used?

A] shear type nibbler

B] punch type nibbler

C] circular cutting machine

D] guillotine shearing machine

23] Scribers are made of...

A] Mild steel

B] High carbon steel

C] Brass

D] Cast iron

24] The size of an engineer's vice is specified by the...

A] Length of the movable jaw

B] Width of the jaws

C] Height of the vice

D] Maximum opening of the jaws

Bench Vice

25] The form of thread used in carpenters vice is...

A] Square

B] Acme thread

C] Sawtooth Thread

D] Knuckle thread

26] The convexity of files helps...

A] To file concave surfaces

B] To file convex surfaces

C] To prevent rounding of edges of work

D] The file to become straight when pressure is applied

27]] Name the instrument used to check the perpendicularity of the branch pipe with the main pipe of a pipe T joint

A] protractor

B] try square

C] spirit level

D] straight edge

28] The caliper meant for measuring the width of a slot is...

A] Odd leg caliper

B] Outside caliper

C] Jenny caliper

D] Inside calliper

29] The included angle of the groove of 'V' block is always....

A] 45◦

B] 60◦

C] 90◦

D] 120◦

'V' blocks

30] 'V' blocks are available in grades of...

A] A & B

B] A,B & C

C] 1,2 & 3

D] 1 & 2

31] 'V' blocks of grade 'B' are made of

A] Cast iron

B] Mild steel

C] Steel

D] Cast steel

32] 'V' block 50/5-40 A is used for holding jobs of diameter

A] Ø 50 mm

B] Ø 5 to Ø 50 mm

C] Ø 5 to Ø 40 mm

D] Ø 40 mm

33] The reason for using cast iron in making 'V' blocks

A] to increase the weight of the block

B] to reduce the cost

C] to reduce the friction

D] to get a good appearance

34] For cutting thin tubing, the most suitable pitch of the hacksaw blade is...

A] 1.8mm

B] 1.4mm

C] 1mm

D] 0.8mm

35] For cutting solid brass, the most suitable pitch of the hacksaw blade is...

A] 1.8mm

B] 1.4mm

C] 1mm

D] 0.8mm

36] A new hacksaw blade after a few strokes becomes loose because of the...

A] Stretching of the blade

B] Wing-nut threads being worn out

C] Wrong pitch of the blade

D] Improper selection of the set of saws.

37] While cutting small diameter pipes, it is advisable to watch regularly and ensure that...

A] The cut is along the curved line

B] More saw teeth are in contract

C] The work is not overheated

D] Proper balancing of hacksaw is maintained

Drilling in Automobile Engineering

38] If the drill runs untrue, it will

A] get too hot

B] cut undersize

C] distort the spindle

D] cut an oversized hole

39] Running the drill too fast many result in

A] spoiling the cutting edge

B] poor surface finish

C] twisting the tang

D] drilling an oval hole

40] A drill with worn land will

A] drill hole oversize

B] drill hole undersize

C] run out of centre

D] drill an accurate hole

41] The morse taper provided on drills used on lathe ranges between

A] MT1 to MT5

B] MT1 to MT4

C] MT0 to MT5

D] MT0 to MT4

42] Feeding the small drill too fast into the work may result in

A] breaking the drill

B] bending the drill

C] cutting an oval shape hole

D] increased production

43] The drill size for a M 20 tap is

A] 17.5 mm

B] 18 mm

C] 18.5 mm

D] 19 mm

44] The taper shank drills are held on the machine by means of...

A] Chucks

B] Sleeves

C] Drift

D] Vice

45] Drill chucks are fitted on the drilling machine spindle by means of a...

A] Knurled ring

B] Arbor

C] Drift

D] Pinion and key

Drill Chuck

46] The Morse taper provided on drills ranges between...

A] <u>MT 1 to MT 5</u>

B] MT 1 to MT 4

C] MT 0 to MT 5

D] MT 0 to MT 4

47] A drift is used for...

A] Drawing a drill location

B] Fixing chuck on the machine spindle

C] Removing a broken drill from the work

D] <u>Removing the drill from the machine spindle</u>

48] When the taper shank of the drill is larger than the machine spindle, the device to hold the drill is a...

A] Drill sleeve

B] <u>Taper socket</u>

C] Drill drift

D] Chuck and key

49] A special feature of the radial drilling machine is...

A] It can be used for drilling with a H.S.S] drill

B] Table can be moved and set at any position

C] A variety of speeds is available

D] The spindle can be brought to any position

50] The point angle of drills depends on...

A] The size of the drill

B] The type of machine

C] The material of the work

D] The RPM of the drill

51] The point angle for a standard drill is...

A] 60°

B] 108°

C] 118°

D] 135°

52] The helical angle determines the...

A] Cutting angle

B] Chew angle

C] Rake angle

D] Lip angle

53] The clearance angle of the drill is between...

A] 3° to 5°

B] 8° to 12°

C] 12° to 20°

D] 15° to 20°

54] The relief angle provided behind the cutting edge is called the..

A] Point angle

B] Chisel edge angle

C] Helix angle

D] Clearance angle

55] A set of number drill series consists of drills in the following ranges] Indicate the correct range

A] 1 to 40

B] 1 to 50

C] 1 to 80

D] 1 to 100

56] In the number drill series, the smallest drill size is...

A] 0.1 mm

B] <u>0.35 mm</u>
C] 0.5 mm
D] 0.52 mm
57] In the number drill series, the largest drill size is...
A] 102 mm
B] <u>5.791 mm</u>
C] 5.613 mm
D] 5.410 mm
58] In the letter drill series, the size of the drill 'A' is equal to ...
A] 13 mm
B] 6.08 mm
C] 6.045 mm
D] <u>5.944 mm</u>
59] In the letter drill series, the largest drill size is equal to...
A] 10.33 mm
B] <u>10.490 mm</u>
C] 12.01 mm
D] 15.00 mm
60] In a remote place (no electricity available] a rail track is to be drilled] Choose the right drilling machine
A] Radial drilling machine
B] Pillar drilling machine
C] <u>Ratchet drilling machine</u>
D] Sensitive drilling Machine
61] A drilling machine used by a carpenter for cabinet making is a...
A] Ratchet drilling machine
B] Radial drilling machine
C] <u>Breast drilling machine</u>
D] Sensitive drilling machine
62] Surface plates are made of...
A] High grade cast steel
B] <u>Fine-grained cast iron</u>
C] Alloy steels
D] Wrought iron
63] The drill size for a M 20 tap is
A] <u>17.5 mm</u>
B] 18 mm
C] 18.5 mm

D] 19 mm

64] Tapping is mostly done to produce

A] external 'V' thread

B] internal 'V' thread

C] external square thread

D] internal square thread

65] The drill size for tapping is

A] more than the tap size

B] less than the tap size

C] equal to the tap size

D] either more or less than the tap size

66] which one of the following is the most suitable tap for lathe work?

A] spiral tap

B] machine tap

C] hand tap

D] left hand tap

67] A die is turned with a

A] die wrench

B] diestock

C] die plate

D] die handle

68] A tumbler gear unit has

A] a single gear

B] two gears

C] three gears

D] four gears

69] The cutting edge of a solid tool is made of

A] carbon steel

B] mild steel

C] super high speed steel

D] stelite

70] The tip of a cemented carbide threading tool is

A] brazed

B] welded

C] soldered

D] clamped to the shank

71] Tool will rub against the work surfaces and the cutting force increases when..

A] The clearance angle is more

B] The clearance angel is less

C] The rake angle is more

D] The rake angle is less

72] Formation of a chip while cutting is based on the...

A] Rake angle of the tool

B] Clearance angle of the tool

C] Wedge angle of the tool

D] Clearance and wedge angle of the tool

73] The suitable cutting fluid for drilling mild steel in a drilling machine is...

A] Synthetic soluble oil

B] Neat oil

C] Distilled water

D] Soluble oil

74] Centre drilling is an operation of...

A] Drilling and countersinking

B] Drilling and counter boring

C] Marking the centre location before drilling

D] Enlarging the diameter of a hole

75] Shaft ends are centre drilled for...

A] Supporting jobs between centres

B] Lubricating the dead centre

C] Reducing the weight

D] Assisting counter boring

76] The Centre drill size is selected on the basis of the

A] length of the job

B] material of the job

C] diameter of the job

D] type of operation

77] Centre drilling is done at a

A] high spindle speed with a high feed

B] low spindle speed with a high feed

C] high spindle speed with a low feed

D] low spindle speed with a low feed

Measuring Instruments in Automobile Engineering

78] The least count of vernier caliper is

A] 0.01 mm

B] 0.02mm
C] 0.001 mm
D] 0.2 mm

Vernier Caliper

79] The graduations of a depth micrometer are...

A] Similar to an outside micrometer

B] In the reverse direction to that of the outside micrometer, both Thimble and sleeve

C] In the reverse direction only on the sleeve

D] In the direction only on the thimble

Depth Micrometer

80] The process of enlarging the end of a hole for accommodating the socket screw head is...

A] Reaming

B] Spot facing

C] Counter boring

D] Counter sinking

Boring Operation

81]While choosing a boring tool for boring a given diameter, select

A] a long tool

B] a short tool

C] a long and stout tool

D] a short and stout tool

82] The cutting edge of the boring tool should be set for a small hole so that it is

A] 0.5 mm above the center

B] 0.5 mm below the center

C] 1 mm above the center

D] in the exact center

83] Bored holes are to be chamfered by using

A] a drill

B] triangular scraper

C] a cranked boring tool

D] a flat file

84] The tool used for boring deep holes is a

A] lathe mandrel

B] sleeve

C] drill

D] boring bar

E] auger bit

85] The cutting speed for rough boring is the

A] same as rough turning

B] same as drilling

C] same as knurling

D] same as thread cutting

86] The reamer is used for...

A] Drilling holes in thin sheets

B] Drilling deep holes

C] Removing burrs

D] Enlarging and finishing holes

Reamer

87] The reamer teeth are unevenly spaced because...

A] They are easy to manufacture

B] They can reduce chattering

C] They help to cut metal gradually

D] They help to remove the reamer easily

88] Which among the following is not a capability of reamers?

A] Finishing small holes

B] Finishing any machined profiles

C] Accuracy to closer limits

D] Producing high quality surface finish

89] The most important quality of any cutting fluid is

A] emulsification

B] specific heat

C] specific gravity

D] viscosity

Cutting Fluid

90] By using coolants on workpieces we can choose

A] higher cutting speeds

B] lower cutting feeds

C] lower cutting speeds

D] heavy depth of cuts

91] The cutting speed for aluminium with H.S.S] tools is

A] 30 m/min

B] 50 m/min

C] 70 m/min

D] 130 m/min

92] The cutting speed for brass with a H.S.S] tool is

A] 10 m/min

B] 25 m/min

C] 70 m/min

D] 140 m/min

93] The distance, which the cutting edge of a tool passes over the material in a minute while machining is Know as...

A] RPM

B] Feed

C] Machine speed

D] Cutting speed

94] The cutting angle for chipping cast iron is...

A] 37.5°

B] 55°

C] 60°

D] 90°

95] The depth of cut is given by

A] the top slide
B] the cross-slide
C] the compound slide
D] adjusting the tool
96] For mounting a lathe chuck
A] start it by hand and then turn the power on
B] mount it on by power
C] mount it by hand
D] mount it with the help of a hammer

Lathe Four Jaw Chuck

97] The morse taper provided on drills used on lathe ranges between
A] MT1 to MT5
B] MT1 to MT4
C] MT0 to MT5
D] MT0 to MT4
98] Feeding the small drill too fast into the work may result in
A] breaking the drill
B] bending the drill

C] cutting an oval shape hole

D] increased production

99] Number of flutes in a twist drills are --------

A] 1

B] 2

C] 3

D] 4

100] Which one of the following drilling machines is used for drilling holes where electricity is not available?

A] Bench drilling machine

B] Pillar drilling machine

C] Redial drilling machine

D] Ratchet drilling machine

101] Which one of the following drilling machine is used for heavy duty work?

A] Bench drilling machine

B] Pillar drilling machine

C] Radial drilling machine

D] Electric hand drilling machine

102] The suitable cutting fluid for drilling mild steel in a lathe is

A] synthetic soluble oil

B] neat cutting oil

C] distilled water

D] soluble oil+water

103] The suitable cutting fluid for precision grinding is

A] Soluble oil

B] Synthetic soluble oil

C] Neat oil

D] Servo Cut's'

Grinding Wheel

104] Advantage of using cutting fluid during grinding operation is ------
A] 5000 surface finish
B] Reduction in cutting forces
C] Reduction in hardening of the work piece
D] All of these]
105] Lubricant is necessary to ....]
A] run the machine smoothly taking least load
B] Run the machine quickly
C] Stop the machine immediately
D] Produce work piece of greater accuracy
106] The main purpose for using a lubricant in machine tools is to ------
A] Cool down the making parts
B] Prevent machine tool from heating
C] Wet the making parts for close contact
D] Minimize the friction between the making parts
107] Driving plates are used for
A] mounting fixtures and workpieces
B] driving shafts between Centre's with a lathe dog
C] facing operations only
D] internal operations only
108] Balancing is done in the face plate work
A] to increase the speed
B] to reduce the pressure on the tool
C] for uniform rotation of work
D] to get a good finish
109] A face plate is used to hold
A] a round job
B] a finished job
C] an irregular Job
D] a hollow job
110] Which is correct angle plate used with face plate
(A] Solid Type
(B] Box Type
(C] Adjustable Type
(D] None of them

Angle Plate

111] Face plate is made from.....]

(A] Mild Steel

(B] Cast Iron

(C] Brass

(D] Aluminium

112] Which following accessories is use for odd an uneven job turning?

(A] Three Jaw Chuck

(B] Two Jaw Chuck

(C] Driving Plate

(D] Face Plate

113] An irregular shaped work piece is turned on a Lathe] Which one of the following work holding accessories is used?

A] Two Jaw chuck

B] Three Jaw chuck

C] Driving plate

D] Face plate

114]The pads of a steady rest are made of

A] carbon steel

B] lead

C] mild steel

D] brass

Steady Rest

115] A steady rest is used

A] to hold jobs

B] for face plate work

C] to drive the job

D] to support the job

116] A follower steady is held on the

A] lathe bed

B] lathe carriage

C] lathe spindle

D] tailstock

117] When turning long work pieces, the following is used

A sleeve

B change gear

C steady rest

D bracket]

118] Knurling operation is done at the

A] turning spindle speed

B] high spindle speed

C] 1/3 of the turning spindle speed

D] 1⁄2 of the turning spindle speed

Knurling Tool

119] Knurling is the operation of

A] shearing

B] forming

C] turning

D] pressing

120] Mandrels are generally used when machining with

A] heavy cuts

B] short facing cuts

C] light cuts

D] boring tools

Limit Fit & Tolerances in Automobile Engineering

121] In the B.I.S system 25 hole deviations are specified by

A] small letters

B] small letters with numbers

C] small letters with tolerance

D] capital letters

122] The standard range of sizes covered in the B.I.S] system of limits and fits are

A] 0 to 10 mm

B] 0 to 100 mm

C] 25 to 400 mm

D] 0 to 500 mm

123] The basic size is the size

A] mentioned in the drawing

B] machined by the operator

C] based on which deviations are given

D] given by the instructor

124] Limits of size are

A] 2

B] 3

C] 4

D] 5

125] The number of fundamental deviations in the B.I.S] system are

A] 20

B] 22

C] 25

D] 28

126] The number of grade of tolerances in the B.I.S] system are

A] 12

B] 16

C] 18

D] 20

127] The size based on which the dimensional deviations are given is called...

A] Actual size

B] Basic size

C] Minimum limit of size

D] Maximum limit of Size

128] The size of parts made by .....] for provide interchange ability properties] (A] Measurement System

(B] Trial and Error System

(C] Limit and Tolerance System

(D] None of Them

129] Your job taper is correct if it is measured

A above the higher limit

B in between higher and lower limit

C below the lower limit]

130] When tolerance given in one side of the basic dimension, it is called --------

A].Tolerance system

B] Unilateral tolerance

C] Bilateral tolerance

D] Allowance System

131] A dimension is stated as (025 H7 in a drawing] The lower limit is -----------

A] 24.75 mm

B] 24.85 mm

C] 25.00 mm

D] 25-021 mm

132] The measured Size Of the dimensions of a component as called---------

A] Basic size

B] Nominal Size

C] Allowed size

D] Actual size

133] In the drawing the dimensions of a shaft is shown 40i 0068/0042, which is the size of Shaft within the tolerance?

A] 4.0.64 mm

B] 40.042 mm

C] 40.000 mm

D] 39.998 mm

134] In Hole basic system ----------

A] The size of the shaft is made constant

B] The Size of the hole is made constant

C] Only 'allowance is given on the hole

D] The permissible tolerance are given on the hole and the Shaft

135] The Size of a component is given as 24 -0.1] What does -O.1 indicates? _

A] Upper deviation is + 0.1 mm]

B] Lower deviation is 0.0 mm

C] Fundamental deviation is 0.0 mm

D] Lower deviation is _0.1 mm

136] The tolerance of a hole iS the difference between the -------

A] Maximum hole Size and maximum Shaft size

B] Maximum hole size and maximum hole Size

C] Minimum'hole size and maximum Shaft Size

D] Minimum hole Size and minimum shaft Size

137] A hole whose lower deviation is zero is called basic hole] Which one of the following letter indicates basic hole?]

A] E

B] F

C] G '

D] H

138] Which one having upper deviation zero?

A] Bassc Shaft

B] Basic hole

C] Tolerance

D] Clearance

139] A ball bearing on a shaft is type of fit? ,

A] Clearance fit

B] Driving fit

C] Shrinkage fit

D] None of the above

140] Which one of the following is important factor required to achieve the interchange ability in mass production?]

A] Geometrical accuracy]

B] Standardization

C] Dimensional accuracy

D] Surface finish

141] In the BIS system of limits and fits, the grade of tolerance are represented by number Symbols and there are ---------i

A] 14 grades of tolerance

B] 16 grades of tolerance

C] 18 grades of tolerance ‘

D] 20 grades of tolerance

142] A Product is said to have the quality when ....]

A] Its shape and dimensions are within the limit

B] It is fit for use

C] It appears to be very good

D] The choice of material is right

143] The maximum clearance required between hole’30 +0.021, 0.000 and shaft 30 -0.110, 0.143 is.

A] 0.110 mm ‘

B]0.131 mm

C] 0.164 mm

D] 0.143 mm

144] A dimension is stated as 25 .1002 mm in a drawing] What is the tolerance?

A] +0.02 mm’

B] +0.04 mm

C] -0.02 mm

D] 25.00 mm

145] A pin is fitted in a hole] The tolerance zone of the pin is entirely above that of hole] The fit obtained will be?

A] Clearance fit

B] Transition fit

C] Interference fit

D] Running fit

146] Interchange ability is normally applied for? _

A] Repairing of parts

B] Mass production

C] Single piece production

D] All of these

147] Tolerance is given to the part size to...........]

A] Production the part within the required permissible size error

B] Increase the production

C] Decrease the Production

D] Finish the components approximately

148] Which one of the following is the clearance fit under the whole basic system?

A] 20 H7/p6'

B] 2067/211

C] ZOG/gll]

D] 20H/g11]

149] The three classes of fits as per BIS system aré ....] ~]

A] Clearance fit, interference fit and transition fit

B] Medium fit, push fit and tight fit

C] Flat fit, round fit and square fit

D] 'Sliding fit ', loose fit and shrinkage fit

150] Which one of the following tolerance specifications has a maximum dimensionless than 20 mm?

A] 20 +0.2,-0.3

B] 20 320.2

C] 20 -0.2, 0.3 e

D]m 20 +500, ~03

151] Difference between the maximum and minimum limit is -~-~~~~-~~~~~ '

A] Single informant

B] Basic shaft

C] Clearance

D] Tolerance

152] A shaft 55 running freely in bush bearing the type of fit is ---------

A] Clearance fit

B] Driving plate

C] shrinkage fit

D] None of the above

153] The taper ratio of the morse taper is

A] 1 in 10

B] 1 in 15

C] 1 in 20

D] 1 in 25

154] The morse standard taper is available in

A] 16 Nos

B] 12 Nos

C] 10 Nos

D] 8 Nos

155] Taper turning by offsetting the tailstock method can produce

A] an internal taper

B] an internal taper thread

C] an external taper

D] both external and internal tapers

Taper by Tailstock Offset

156] By using the taper turning attachment, tapers can be turned with a setting angle up to

A] 10◦

B] 15◦

C] 20◦

D] 30◦

157] The accuracy of a taper is generally checked by means of……

A] taper gauges

B] gauge blocks

C] indicator and height gauge

D] 'V' blocks

158] Turning tapers by the compound rest method involves working solely with

Decimal measurements

B fractional measurements

C metric measurements

D angular measurements]

159] Long tapers are produced

A with the taper turning attachment

B with the compound slide

C by setting over the tail stock

D by adjusting the cross slide]

160] The length of turned tapers are checked with

A vernier calliper

B micrometer

C inside callper

D dial test indicator]

161] The disadvantages of taper turning using the com] pound slide are

A] only long tapers can be turned

B] only very large tapers can be turned

C] only manual in feed is possible

D] only short tapers can be turned due to the restrictions of the compound slide]

162] External tapers are checked with

A] limit plug gauge

B] taper ring gauge

C]taper plug gauge

D] thread plug gauge]

163] The use of a taper turned on lathe is ----

A] Assist to transmit drive in the assembled parts

B] Used for Assembly and disassembly of parts

C] Give self alignment in the assembled parts

164] Which type of method is used in mass production of production of producing small length of taper?

A] Form tool

B] Compound slide

C] Tailstock offset.

D] Taper turning attachment

165] Morse standard taper is one of the internationally accepted standards taper, which is available in numbers from--------

A]1to7

B]1 to 8

C] O to 7

D] 0 to 8

166] Which taper turning method is used for cutting steep taper?

A] Set over method

B] Taper turning attachment

C] Form tool

D] Swivelling the compound rest

167] Morse taper is used in which of the following machine components -...

A] Spindles of lathe

B] Spindles of drill machine

C] Shanks of reamers

D] All of these

168] For mass production of the taper which one of the following method is used.......]

A] Tailstock offset method

B] Taper turning attachment method

C] Form too method

D] Compound slide method

169] The major diameter of the taper is 40 mm, minor diameter is 30 mm] The total length of the job is 100 mm is tapered then offset is given by -

A] 5 mm

B] 7.5 mm

C] 12 mm

D] 9 mm

170] The accuracy of an ordinary bevel protractor is --' ------------degree]

A] One

B] Three

C] Two

D] Four

171] The least count of a vernier bevel protractor is...

A] 1”

B] 5’

C] 1◦

D] 5 ◦

172] The part of a vernier bevel protractor which is normally used as a reference base for measuring angles is the...

A] Blade

B] Stock

C] Disc

C] Main scale

173] The part of a vernier bevel protector on which main scale divisions are marked is the...

A] Stock

B] Dial

C] Disc

D] Adjustable blade

174] The part of a bevel protractor, which comes in contact with the inclined surface while measuring is the...

A] Blade

B] Stock

C] Disc

D] Dial

175] The value of each division of the main scale of a vernier bevel protractor is...

A] 5’

B] 1◦

C] 5◦

D.10◦

176] The value of each division of the vernier scale of a bevel protractor is...

A] 1◦

B] 1◦5’

C] 1◦55’

D.5'

177] The part of the vernier bevel protractor on which main scale divisions are marked

A stock

B dial

C disc

D adjustable blade

178] In Vernier bevel protractor is designed to measure?

A] Acute angles

B] Obtuse angles

C] Acute and Obtuse angle

D] Liner dimensions

179] To get least count of 5 in a vernier bevel protractor the 23° main scale are divided into -..

A] 12 equal parts on vernier scale

B] 22 equal parts on vernier scale

C] 24 equal parts on vernier scale

D] 25 equal parts on vernier scale

180] Which of the following is not the part of a combination set?

A] Stock

B] Square head

C] Protractor head

D] Centre head

181] The datum, form which the measurements of the vernier height gauge are taken, is...

A] The beam

B] The vernier slide

C] The base

D] Above the scriber poing

Vernier Height Gauge

182]The part of a vernier height gauge on which the main scale divisions are graduated is the...

A] Base

B] Beam

C] Fine setting device

D] The vernier plate

183] On which part of the vernier height gauge are the main scale division graduated?]

A] Base

B] Vernier plate

C] Beam

D] Fine adjusting unit

184] For marking purpose a Vernier height gauge must be on the --------

A] Bed of a machine tool

B] Surface plate

C] Square block

D] Any flat surface

185] Before using Vernier height gauge make sure that the --------

A] Locking screw is in a locked position

B] Scriber is Locked

C] Zero of the vernier coincides with zero of the main scale

D] Gib is Provided

186] The least count Of a vernier height gauge is...........]

A] 0.05 mm

B] 0.1 mm

C] 0.02 mm

D] 0001 mm

187] Which laying out the vernier height gauge must be used on the ----------

A] V block

B] Machine bed

C] Surface plate

D] Any flat surface

188] The part which is slides on the beam of a vernier height gauge is known as a ------

A] Base

B] Beam scale

C] Scriber

D] Vernier slide

189] The base of the vernier height gauge is generally made out of ---------

A] Cast iron]

B] Steel

C] Aluminium alloy

D] Tungsten carbide

190] Which instrument iis used for marking layout?

A] Micrometer

B] Vernier

C] Depth gauge

D] Vernier height gauge

191] While marking with a Vernier height gauge, the work piece is generally ----------

A] Supported by an angle plate

B] Supported by another work piece

C] Held by one hand

D] Held without support

192] Which of the following is not the part of a combination set?

A] Stock

B] Square head

C] Protractor head

D] Centre head

Engineering Drawing in Automobile Engineering

18]The 'T' square is used for drawing lines ......

a] inclined

b] curved

c] vertical
d] horizontal
19] For drawing large size circle is drawn by.....
a] straight bar
b] lengthening bar
c] big bar
d] small bar
20] To draw or measure angle is used by.....
a]set square
b] protractor
c] 'T' square
d] none of these
21] The grade of pencil is used to sketching lettering ....
a] conical point
b] chisel point
c] soft
d] low
22] For drawing thin lines of uniform thickness the pencil should be sharpened in the form of ....
a] chisel edge
b]conical
c] pointed
d] none of these
23] What is used for drawing curves which can not drawn by compass
a] small compass
b] French curve
c] protractor
d] none of these
24]Unnecessary lines is removed by .....
a] Duster
b] sand paper block
c] eraser
d] none of these
25] Circle and arcs are drawn by means of .....l.
a] compass
b] divider
c] lengthening bar
d]none of these

26] Inking pen is used in drawing ......

a] horizontal line

b] non circular arcs

c] vertical lines

d] all of these

27] The card board scale are available in set of .....

a] 7

b] 8

c] 6

d] 9

28] The convenient length size of 30 -60°-90° set square for used in school and colleges are......

a] 250

b] 200

c] 300

d] none of these

29] Drawing board is shape of ....

a] square

b] rectangular

c] triangular

d] none of these

30] The 'T' square , set square ,scale protractor are complain use in.......

a] protractor

b] mini drafter

c] set square

d] none of these

31]Set square , T square edges are bevelled for the purpose of....

a] curve line

b] inking lines

b] taking measurements

d] none of these

32]Geometrical construction which are mostly based on plane geometry and which are very.......

a] Accuracy

b] Quality

c] Essential

d] Superior quality

33] How much method of drawing the regular polygons.......

a] Inscribe circle method and arc method
b] General method for drawing any polygon
c] Alternative method
d] All of these

34] The line AB can be divided into .... equal parts.
a] 7
b] 10
c] 15
d] All of them

35] Which method of constructing triangl in circle......
a] Inscribing
b] Describing
c] Both a and b
d] None of these

36] When two sides of the hexagon are required to be horizontal the starting point for stepping equal division should be on an end of the.....
a] Horizontal diameter
b] Vertical diameter
c] Inclined diameter
d] None of these

37] If two sides of hexagon are required to be vertical the starting point should be on an end of the....
a] Inclined diameter
b] Horizontal diameter
c] Vertical diameter
d] None of these

38] The section obtained by the inter section of the right circular cone by a plane in different position relative to the axis of the cone are called.......
a] Conics
b] Circles
c] Triangles
d] Half circle

39] When the section plane is inclined to the axis and cuts all the generators on one side on a apex the section is in......
a] Conic section
b] Ellipse
c] Parabola
d] Hyperbola

40] When the section plane is inclined to the axis and is parallel to one of the generators the section is a ....

a] Ellipse

b] Parabola

c] Hyperbola

d] Cycloid

41] Use of elliptical curve is........

a] Arches

b] Dams and monuments

c] Manholes, gland & stuffing boxes

d] All of these

42] Use of parabolic curve is.........

a] Bridges & arches

b] Sound reflectors

c] Light reflectors

d] All of these

43] Use of hyperbolical curve is......

a] Cooling towers and water channel

b] Dames

c] Bridges

d] All of these

44] When the point is within the circle, the curve is called an.......

a] Superior trochoid

b] Interior trochoid

c] Trochoid

d] Isotrochoid

45] When the point outside the circle then the curve is called as......

a] Interior trochoid

b] Superior trochoid

c] Trochoid

d] Insuperior trochoid

46] The curve general by a point on a circumference of a circle, which rolls without slipping along another circle it is called.......

a] Epicycloids

b] Hypocycloid

c] Involute

d] None of these

47] When the circle rolls inside another circle the curve is called.......

a] Hypocycloid
b] Epicycloids
c] Trochoid
d] Hypotrochoid
48] The use of archemedian spiral curve is made in........
a] Teeth profiles of helical gears
b] Profiles of cams
c] Both a & b
d] None of these
49] The cams are widely used in........
a] Automates
b] Printing machines
c] C engines
d] All of these
50] Spring index =
a] Diameter of coil / diameter of a wire
b] Diameter of wire /diameter of coil
c] Mean diameter of wire / diameter of coil
d] Mean diameter of a coil / diameter of wire
51] Eccentricity =
a] Distance of a point from the focus / distance of the point from directrix
b] Distance of focus from point / distance of point from
c] Distance of point from focus / distance of directrix of point
d] Distance of point from directrix / distance of point from focus
52] Mathematically an ellipse can be described by equation.....
a] $a^2 / X^2 + y^2 / b^2 = 1$
b] $x^2 / a^2 + y^2 / b^2$
c] $x^2 / a^2 + y^2 / b^2 = 0$
d] $x^2 / a^2 + y^2 / b^2 = 1$
53] Mathematically a parabola can be described by an equation......
a] $y^2 = 4ax$
b] $x^2 = 2ay$
c] $x^2 = 4ay$
d] Both a & b
54] Mathematically hyperbola can be described by an equation.......
a] $x^2 /a^2 - y^2 /b^2 = 1$
b] $x^2 /y^2 - y^2 /x^2 = 0$

c] Both a & b
d] None of these
55] Cycloid can be described by an equation......
a] y = a(1-cos Ø]
b] x = a(Ø -sin Ø]
c] Both a & b
d] None of these
56] The mathematically represented hypocycloid is.....
a] Y = a $\cos^3$ Ø, X = a $\sin^3$ Ø
b] X = a $\sin^3$ Ø, Y = a $\cos^3$ Ø
c] X = a $\cos^3$ Ø, Y = a $\sin^3$ Ø
d] None of these
57] Mathematically represented by involute is
a] X = r sin Ø - r Ø cos Ø, Y = r cos + r Ø sin Ø
b] X = r sin Ø + r cos Ø, Y = r cos Ø – r Ø sin Ø
c] Y = r Ø cos Ø – r sin Ø, X = r sin Ø – r Ø cos Ø
d] X = r cos Ø + r Ø sin Ø, Y =r sin Ø - r Ø cos Ø
58] The lines from the object to the plane are called.......
a] Projection
b] Projector
c] Reference plane
d] None of these
59] The orthographic projection an object is represented by View on the mutual perpendicular projection lines
a] Two or three
b] Three or two
c] Three or four
d] None of these
60] When the projectors are parallel to each other & also perpendicular to the plane, the projection is called......
a] Isometric projection
b] Oblique projection
c] Orthographic projection
d] Perspective projection
61] The two planes employed for the purpose of Orthographic projections are......
a] Auxillary plane
d] Horizontal plane

c] Reference plane

d] None of these

62] The line in which they intersect is termed the reference line & is denoted by the letters.......

a] AB

b] YZ

c] XY

d] None of these

63] The projection on the VP is called........

a] Side view

b] Front view

c] Top view

d] All of these

64] ....Method, when the views are drawn in their relative positions, the plane comes below the elevation. The view of the object as observed from the left-side the right of elevation.

a] Plane of projection

b] First angle projection

c] Third angle projection

d] None of these

65] Third angle projection method, the object is assumed to be situated in the........ quadrant.

a] First quadrant

b] Second quadrant

c] Third quadrant

d] Fourth quadrant

66] .... Method of projection is used in U.S.A & also in other countries.

a] plane of projection

b] Orthographic projection

c] First-angle projection

d] Third angle projection

67] When an object is situated on the ground, in first angle projection method, the bottom of its ..... will co-inside with XY

a] Top view

b] Front view

c] side view

d] All of these

68] The important element of this projection system

a] An object

b] Plane of projection

c] An observer

d] All of these

69] When line AB is parallel to HP hence ....

a] It' front view to AB

b] It''s side view equal to AB

c] It's top view equal to AB

d] None of these

70] When a line is parallel to a plane; it's projection on plane is equal to it's ;

a] True length

b] True shape

c] True size

d] None of these

71] The point is parallel in which the line or line produced meet the point is plane is called it's ....

a] Line

b] ratio

c] Trace

d] none of these

72] .... is the shortest distance between two points.

a] a line

b] a point

c] a straight line

d] none of these

73] When the line intersect horizontal plane that's called.....

a] horizontal trace

b] vertical trace

c] trace of line

d] none of these

74]Planes may be divided into two main types ......

a] Perpendicular planes, auxillary planes

b] Perpendicular plane, oblique planes

c] Auxillary planes , perpendicular planes

d] none of these

75] Planes which are inclined to the reference plane are called......

a] Auxillary plane
b] obliqeu plane
c] Perpendicular planes
d] picture plane

76] When a plane is perpendicular to a reference plane it's projection on that plane is a..........

a] horizontal line
b] parallel line
c] straight line
d] none of these

77] When a plane is parallel to a reference plane , it's projection on that plane shows........

a] It's true shape &size
b] It's true length & size
c] It's true height & size
d] none of these

78] Plane perpendicular to VP & HP that plane is called as ....

a] Auxillary Plane
b] Oblique Plane
c] Perpendicular Plane
d] None of these

79] Perpendicular plane can be divides into the following types.........

a] Perpendicular to both the reference planes.
b] Perpendicular to one plane & parallel to other
c] Perpendicular to one plane & inclined to other
d] All of these

80] The planes have only two dimensions, viz........

a] Length & breadth
b] Length & height
c] Length & thickness
d] All of these

81] The imaginary line of prism joining the centrs of the bases called.........

a] Faces
b] Axis
c] Apex
d] Base

82] A right & regular prism has it's axis....... to the bases

a] Parallel
b] Perpendicular
c] Inclined
d] None of these

83] When a pyramid or a cone is cut by a plane parallel to it's base thus removing the top portion, the remaining portion is called it's.........

a] Sphere
b] Cone
c] Cylinder
d] Frustum

84] Oblique cylinder & cones have their axes........ to their base

a] Inclined
b] Parallel
c] Perpendicular
d] All of these

85] Projection of two equal sphere s resting on the ground & in contact with each other, with the line joining there centre parallel to the..........

a] A VP
b] VP
c] HP
d] All of these

86] Projections of section on the other plane to which it is inclined is called.......

a] Section planes
b] Apparent section
c] True shape of sphere
d] None of these

87] When the section plane is parallel to the HP or the ground, the true shape of the section will be seen in.........

a] Front view
b] Side view
c] Top view
d] All of these

88] Surface of solid are laid out on a plane the figure obtained is called its........

a] Interpenetration
b] Development
c] Intersection

d] None of these

89] Development of surfaces is essential in.........

a] Foundry shop

b] Sheet metal work

c] Fitting shop

d] None of these

90] Which method of development used in transition pieces?

a] Parallel diameter

b] Radial line method

c] Triangulation method

d] Approximate method

91] Which method of development used in pyramids and cones.........

a] Radial line method

b] Parallel line method

c] Approximate method

d] Triangulation method

92] Parallel line method is used in..........

a] Prism

b] Cylinder

c] Cubes

d] All of these

93] Which method of development used in surface as sphere, paraboloid, ellipsoid, hyperboloid, and helicoids

a] Radial line method

b] Triangulation method

c] Approximate method

d] Parallel line method

94] Zone method and lune method is used in development of........

a] Prisms

b] Cones

c] Sphere

d] Pyramids

95] Calculation the subtended angle Θ by the formula $\Theta = 360^0 \times$ radius of the base circle

a] Length of axis

b] Slant height

c] Radius of axis

d] None of these

96] In engineering practice, objects constructed may have constituent part, the surfaces of which intersect one another in lines called........ of intersection.

a] Lines

b] Cones

c] Cylinder

d] Prisms

97] The line of interaction may be depending upon the nature of.......

a] Intersection surface

b] Intersecting solids

c] Intersection cones

d] None of these

98] The two plane surface intersect in a........ line

a] Curve

b] Straight

c] Plane

d] All of these

99] The line of intersection between two curved surface or between......... Surface and a curved surface is a curve.

a] A curved

b] A plane

c] A solids

d] None of these

100] When a solids completely penetration another solids there will be two lines of intersection. These lines are sometimes called the line or........

a] Line of interpenetration

b] Curve of interpenetration

c] Solids of interpenetration

d] All of these

101] Use of penetration curve is.......

a] Sheet metal work

b] Fitting shop

c] Fabricating work

d] Foundry shop

102] Methods of determining the line of intersection between surface of two interpenetration.........

a] Approximate method & radial line method

b] Line method and cutting plane method

c] Triangulation method and parallel line method

d] None of these

103] Example of interpenetration is..........

a] Two prism intersection

b] Cylinder and prism intersection

c] Cone and cylinders intersection

d] <u>All of these</u>

104] Two cylinder intersection is example of.........

a] <u>Intersection</u>

b] Interpenetration

c] Cone intersection

d] None of these

105] .... Method is explained in detail while solving illustrative problems

a] Line method

b] Radial line method

c] <u>Cutting plane method</u>

d] Parallel line method

106] What is a type of isometric projection?

a] <u>Pictorial projection</u>

b] Orthographic projection

c] Perspective projection

d] Oblique Projection

107] Isometric views have been drawn........

a] Full scale

b] Half scale

c] <u>True length</u>

d] True scale

108] The line parallel to isometric axis are called........

a] Isometric axis

b] <u>Isometric line</u>

c] Isometric planes

d] Isometric views

109] The isometric projection is reduce in the ratio.........

a] 3 :

b] 1 : 2

c] 2 : 2

d] <u>2 : 3</u>

110] The isometric projection of circle drawn with........

a] Isometric Plane

b] Isometric graph

c] Isometric Drawing

d] Isometric Scale

111] The major axis of the ellipse is long than..............

a] Radius of the circle

b] True diameter

c] Diameter of the circle

d] None of these

112] Makes practice for drawing of isometric view using........

a] Isometric planes

b] Isometric lines

c] Isometric graph

d] Isometric view

113] Use of parabolic curve is

a] Sound reflectors

b] Dams

c] Man hole of boiler

d] Gland & stuffing box

114] When the section plane is inclined the true shape of section on

a] AVP

b] VP

c] HP

d] A/P

115] When section plane is perpendicular to both the HP & VP the true shape of section on

a]Top view

b] Side view

c] Front view

d]None of this

116] When view projected on auxiliary planes are called

a] Auxiliary view

b Sectional view

c] Front view

d] None of these

117] Invisible features of an object are shown by means of

a] Outline

b] Chain lines

c] Hidden lines

d] None of these

118] Importance of sectional view on drawing for

a] Internal details

b] Outer details

c] Hatching

d] None of these

119] The component is cut by a straight cutting plane is divided in to two parts

a] Half section

b] Full section

c] Offset section

d] Removed section

120] section line is two different parts (pieces] in contact should be drown in...

a] Same direction

b] Opposite direction

c]parallel direction

d] None of these

121] When area to be sectioned in very small as for this plate and structural members blacked in section may be used. A space of not less than

a] 0.07mm

b] 0.7mm

c] 0.05mm

d] 0.5mm

122] The sum of interior angles of polygon is equal

a] (2*n-4]*Right angle

b] (2*n]*Right angle-4

c] (2*4-n]*Right angle

d] (2-4*n]*Right angle

123] One micron is equal to ....mm

a] 0.001

b] 1000

c] 0.01

d] 0.1

124] Development of surface is essential in.....

a] foundry shop

b] sheet metal work

c] fitting shop

d] none of these

125] Which method of development used in transition piece?

a] parallel line method

b] radial line method

c] triangulation method

d] none of these

126] The isometric projection is reduced in the ratio of

a] √2:√3

b] √3:√2

c] 1:√2

d] none of these

127] When measurements are required in three units the scale is used....

a] full scale

b] plain scale

c] half scale

d] none of these

128]Isometric drawing is larger in production about isometric projection is....

a] 22.5%

b] 0.815

c] 9/11

d] none of these

129] While isometric of sphere of spherical parts.......is must be used.

a] full scale

b] isometric length

c] true length

d] half scale

130] When circle draw with isometric scale the length of major axis of the ellipse to the ....

a] true diameter

b] isometric diameter

c] isometric diameter

d] none of these

131] In isometric view which contain a large number of non –isometric lines which method is used

a] box method

b] off-set method

c] co-ordinate method

d] centre lay out method

132] When drawing is drawn smaller than actual size of object .....

a] full scale

b] enlarging scale

c] reducing scale

d] none of these

133] When e=1 curve is called.....

a] parabola

b] hyperbola

c] ellipse

d] none of these

134]Compare with isometric drawing the advantage of oblique projection is....

a] front face is in true shape

b] two axis are always perpendicular to each othe

c] receding axis is taken at some convenient angles

d] none of these

135]If all the receding edges are drawn true length the oblique projection is called...

a] cavilier projection

b] cabinet projection

c] general projection

d] none of these

136] The large object such as building the point is usually taken height of .....

a] 0.8mm

b] 1.2mm

c] 1.8mm

d] 1.5mm

137] Central plane is the imaginary vertical plane which passes through....

a] P. P

b] H.L

c] G.P

d] C.P

138] When object is parallel to P.P the perspective is called......

a] <u>one point</u>

b] two point

c] three point

d] none of these

139] The line drawn through the station point from the picture plane shall be ....

a] <u>P.A</u>

b] H.L

c] G.L

d] C

140] The distance of the station point from the picture plane shall be .....

a] Max. Diameter of the object

b] <u>Twice the max. Diameter of the object</u>

c] Half the max. Diameter of the object

d] none of these

141] In isometric view of hexagonal plane all the sides of hexagon is .....

a] equal length

b] <u>unequal length</u>

c] none of these

142] When all the faces are equal & regular the polyhedron is said....

a] <u>regular</u>

b] prisms

c] irregular

d] pyramid

143] Oblique prisms &pyramid have ......

a] axis perpendicular to the base

b] <u>axis inclined to the base</u>

c] faces inclined to the H.P

d] none of these

144] Icosahedrons has equal equilateral triangular faces

a] 12

b] 8

c] <u>20</u>

d] 6

145] When a pyramid or cone is cut by a plane parallel to its base is called.....

a] pyramid

b] turned carted

c] frustum

d] none of these

146] Plane which are inclined to both the reference plane is called ......

a] oblique plane

b] perpendicular plane

c] inclined plane

d] none of these

147] When a line parallel to H.P & perpendicular to V.P the trace line is.....

a] V.T

b] H.T

c] no trace

d] V.T& H.T

148] When a line parallel to the V.P and inclined to H.P the true length of line in.....

a] front view

b] top view

c] side view

d] none of these

149] When point situated in front quadrant

a] above the H.P & in front of V.P

b] below the H.P & in front of V.P

c] behind the V.P & above H.P

d] below the H.P & behind the V.P

150] Find the quadrant of point "b" is 15 mm above H.P and 25mm behind the V.P

a] I st

b] III rd

c] IIII th

d] II nd

151] In first angle projection front view is ......

a] above the top view

b] below the top view

c] above the side view

d] below the side view

152] In orthographic projection the projectors are ....

a] parallel to plane

b] perpendicular to plane

c] inclined to plane

d] none of these

153] L.H.S.V means.........

a] length of side view

b] left hand view

c] right hand view

d] left hand side view

154] The object lines between the observer and the plane of projection is ....

a] 3rd angle

b] 1st angle

c] 4th angle

d] 2nd angle

155] In third angle projection plane of projection is assumed to be ......

a] non transparent

b] quadrant

c] transparent

d] dihedral angle

156] In third angle projection top view is always on......

a] above front view

b] above top view

c] below the front view

d] below the side view

157] Four quadrants which may be called as......

a] anticlockwise

b] first and third angle

c] dihedral angles

d] none of these

158] In first angle projection method the view see from the left is placed on .....

a] left of the front view

b] right of front view

c] above the top view

d] below the front view

159] The size of A2 paper is .....

a] 297*420

b] 594*841

c] 420*594

d] 210*297

160] The edge of board on which 'T' square is sli9ding is called ......

a] straight edge

b] working edge

c] chisel edge

d] none of these

161] The size of title block as recommended by B.I.S . is .....

a] 185*65

b] 150*50

c] 170*65

d] none of these

162] For A2 size sheet the number of zones suggested by B.I.S. along the length & width.......

a] 12,8

b] 16,12

c] 8,6

d] none of these

163] The drawing sheet is so folded that...... is always on the top.

a] drawing

b] lettering

c] title block

d] none of these

164] In free hand sketching horizontal lines are sketched from.......

a] right to left

b] up to down

c] left to right

d] none of these

165] When drawing is down smaller than actual size of object

a] enlarging scale

b] reducing scale

c] full scale

d] none of these

166] The ratio of the length of the object represented on drawing to the actual length of object is called.......

a] full scale

b] R.F.

c] half scale

d] plain scale

167] When measurements are required in three unit the scale is used.....
a] full scale
b] half scale
c] plain scale
d] none of these
168] When protractor is not available the scale of chord is used ......
a] measure length
b] measure angle
c] measure scale
d] none of these
169] The least count of a vernier calliper is ....
a] 0.001
b] <u>0.02</u>
c] 0.001
d] 0.0002
170] Which scale is used to read a very small unit with great accuracy?
a] plain scale
b] <u>diagonal scale</u>
c] scale of chord
d] vernier scale
171] The R.F. is greater than one (1] the scale is ....
a] plain scale
b] diagonal scale
c] <u>enlarging scale</u>
d] reducing scale

AutoCAD for Automobile Engineering

1] Which is the latest version of AutoCAD software?
a) 2016
b) 2017
c) <u>2018</u>
d) 2019
2] Which key is used to obtain properties palette in AutoCAD?
a) <u>Control+1</u>
b) Control+2
c) Control+3
d) Control+4
3] AutoCAD was first released in the year:
a) 1858

b) 1966
c) 1898
d) 1982

4] How many units are available in AutoCAD?

a) 4
b) 5
c) 7
d) 6

5] Which mode allows the user to draw 90° straight lines :

a) Osnap
b) Ortho
c) Linear
d) Polar tracking

6] To obtain parallel lines, concentric circles and parallel curves; __________ is used.

a) Array
b) Fillet
c) Copy
d) Offset

7] The default grid spacing in both X and Y directions is:

a) 10
b) 20
c) 5
d) 15

8] How many workspaces are available in AutoCAD?

a) 2
b) 4
c) 3
d) 5

9] Scale command can be accessed easily by typing:

a) SL
b) S
c) SC
d) C

10] Which command is used to divide the object into segments having predefined length?

a) Divide
b) Chamfer

c) Trim
d) Measure

11] How many grip points does a circle have?

a) 5
b) 4
c) 3
d) 2

] When drawing in 2D, what axis do you NOT work with?

A] X
B] Y
C] Z
D] WCS

] The primary difference between the Model tab and the Layout tab(s) is ____.

A] the Model tab is used for drawing in 3D and a Layout is used for drawing in 2D

B] the Model tab is where you create the drawing and a Layout tab represents the sheet that you will plot or print on

C] the color of the background

D] the Model tab displays the drawing you are copying from and the Layout tab is where you lay out the new drawing

] Which of the following is NOT a property of an object

A] Line weight
B] Measure
C] Hyperlink
D] Elevation

] Which command convert discrete objects in polyline

A] Union
B] Subtract
C] Join
D] Polyline

] To print the entire project, you will choose to regulate what to plot

A] Display
B] Extends
C] Limits
D] Window

] What is the usefulness of viewports

A] Allows us to see the screen or on paper different views of the same project

B] Give us the ability to see projects have become a newer version of AutoCAD from our

C] We can make a change in one part of the plan, without affecting the rest

D] None of the above

] What is the difference between the Scale command from the command Zoom

A] Scale for single object, while the Zoom whole plan

B] No difference

C] H Scale can grow / shrink a shape up 10 times, while the Zoom has no limits

D] H Scale changes the size of objects, while the Zoom changes the visibility of the project

] When to fix a block attribute

A] Before you fix the block

B] When I make the block

C] After fix the block

D] No matter the number

] What you cannot create from the command Offset

A] Vertical straight

B] Concentric circles

C] Three parallel lines

D] Parallel arcs

] By what symbol shows the snap point to the closest point

A] with circles and dots in the center

B] With two triangle

C] With three orthogonal

D] With Diamond

] Which state grid is use to design perspective

A] Parametric

B] Isometric

C] Pro-optic

D] Rectangular

] If I want to draw a line in the direction 07:30 (local time) will give an angle

A] -135 degrees

B] 270 degrees

C] -225 degrees

D] None of the above

] When in absolute Cartesian coordinates have points A (10.8) and B (6.5), then to make a line from A -> B with relative polar coordinates will write

A] @ -5 <36.88

B] @ 4 <30

C] @ 5 <216,88

D] @ 3 <60

] What is the minimum allowable number of layers in a drawing

A] 0

B] 5

C] 1

D] 2

] Which of the following is not a keyboard shortcut of AutoCAD?

A] Ctrl + P

B] Alt + F4

C] Ctrl + F4

D] Alt + B

] Why do we have 16,7 M colors in RGB

A] Because so one can distinguish man

B] since this is the limit of graphics cards

C] For each color we have 256 shades and colors combination third

D] Because we want compatibility between PC and Macintosh

] What setting gradient allows us to fill an open area?

A] Gap

B] Tolerance

C] Transparency

D] Open

] What are the various options from left to right and the opposite direction?

A] Choose a different category of objects

B] select objects according to their color

C] Select objects according to their position

D] No difference

] Which is corresponded to zoom mouse wheel?

A] Zoom in / zoom out

B] pan & scan

C] extents / all

D] scale

] What command allows us to select objects based on some status?

A] Properties

B] Qselect

C] Pselect

D] Attributes

] How to make a random line with an angle of 40 degrees to the x axis

A] will write 0 <40

B] will write 2 <40

C] will write 3<40

D] will write 4 <40

] Which of the following file extensions cannot open the AutoCAD

A] dwg

B] dxf

C] dot

D] dws

] A surveyor with a headband to measure the dimensions of a site, he make measurements by

A] No one method

B] Related Cartesian coordinates

C] Absolute polar coordinates

D] None of the above

] What is the command used for Plagiostomi angle?

A] Chamfer

B] Fillet

C] Offset

D] Mirror

] When should I use the Block Editor

A] To write text block

B] To fix outer block

C] To fix dynamic block

D] To store it in another version of AutoCAD

] If the scheme that stores will be opened in AutoCAD 2006 then you must save it in

A] AutoCAD 2004 dwg

B] AutoCAD 2006 dwg

C] AutoCAD 2007 dwg
D] None of the above
] Print scale 1:50 means that
A] The draft is 50 times less expensive than the original
B] A 3 cm corresponds to half a meter
C] A measure corresponds to 50 cm
D] None of the above
29] What do the letters UCS
A] Uniform Calculator System
B] United CAD System
C] Universal CAD Settings
D] Universal Coordinate System

] What is the difference of two regular 8-gonon, which is one inscribed and another circumscribed circle
A] No difference
B] different opening angles
C] different side length
D] different crowd sides

] If during the CCW measurement result gives an angle 135 degrees, the same CW angle measured is
A] 225 degrees
B] -135 degrees
C] -225 degrees
D] 135 degrees

] What does associative hatch
A] Monitors the changes in shape that fills
B] Relates to the other hatch plan
C] Both of the above
D] None of the above

] What is the difference between command Plot and Print
A] plot command prints only big plans
B] The plot command for CNC (CAM)
C] No difference
D] print command can print up to A3 size paper

] If you change the scale list a project that I have started from 1:50 1:10 then

A] You will have to start over

B] You should not raise the objects already exist (scale) by 5

C] You will not need to change anything in hitherto methodology

D] should be converted into new items that will add based on the new scale

] Which of the following is NOT a unit of length measurement?

A] Yards

B] Parsecs

C] Microns

D] Grads

] What does the command Wblock

A] Warp-speed block

B] Write block

C] Window block

D] Wide-area block

] Where should you pay attention when you are working with autocad commands?

A] Drawing area

B] Status bar

C] Tool bars

D] Command window

] Polar coordinates are used mostly for drawing______

A] Arc

B] Ellipse

C] Angular lines

D] None of the above

] How many SNAP points does an object have?

A] 1

B] 4

C] 5

D] Depend on object

] How many points do you need to define for the rectangle command?

A] One

B] Two

C] Three

D] Four

] How many AutoCAD objects are in a rectangle?

A] One

B] Two

C] Three

D] Four

] How will you deselect an object while you are selecting set of objects?

A] Ctrl+ click on the object to be removed

B] Shift + Click on the object to be removed

C] Alt + Click on the object to be removed

D] None of the above

] How long will a line from 0,5 to 5,5 be ________

A] 10 units

B] 5 units

C] 15 units

D] None of the above

] Objects are rotated around the

A] Bottom of the object

B] Base point

C] Center of the object

D] Origin

] The origin of a drawing is at

A] 0,0

B] 1,0

C] 0,1

D] 1,1

] How would you select set of objects in a drawing?

A] By a crossing window drawn from right to left

B] By a crossing window drawn left to right

C] Shift+ clicking on the objects

D] None of the above

] Fillet command can be used to obtain__________

A] Sharp corners

B] Round corners

C] Both of the above

D] None of the above

] A polar array creates new objects_____

A] In a grid pattern

B] In a circular pattern

C] In a straight line

D] All of the above

] How many layers a drawing should have?

A] 1

B] 2

C] As many as depending on the complexity

D] None of the above

] Scaling objects make them_______

A] Smaller

B] Bigger

C] Either smaller or bigger

D] None of the above

Electrical MCQ for Automobile Engineering

85] A heater draws a current of 8A when connected to a 240V source] What is the resistance value of the heater element in ohms?

A] 40

B] 20

C] 30

D] 60

86] An electric soldering iron with an 80 ohms heating element is plugged into a 240V outlet] How much current will be drawn by the iron?

A] 2A

B] 3A

C] 4A

D] 5A

87] The alternator in a car delivers 4A and has a load of 3 ohms connected across its terminals] Find the voltage of the circuit

A] 18V

B] 24V

C] 12V

D] 16V

88] Three resistors of 1K ohms, 2K ohms and 7K ohms are connected in series with a 30 V supply] If 2 K ohms and 7 K ohms resistors are open circuited, a voltmeter connected across the 7K ohms resistor will indicate...

A] 10 k ohms, 3A

B] 10 k ohms, 300mA

C] 10 k ohms, 3 mA

D] 5 k ohms, 6 mA

89] A voltage source produces an IR drop of 40V across a 20 ohms resistance, 60V across a 30 ohms resistance and 180V across a 90 ohms resistance all in series] How much is the applied voltage?

A] 180 V

B] 240 V

C] 100 V

D] 280 V

90] Three resistors 27 ohms, 47 ohms and 68 ohms are connected in parallel] What is the otal resistance?

A] less than 27 ohms

B] greater than 68 ohms

C] between 27 and 47 ohms

D] sum of all the three resistances

91] One million and one mege ohms resistors are there if connected both in parallel, what would be the combined resistance value?

A] 0.5 mega ohm

B] 0.5 milli ohm

C] 0.5 kilo ohm

D] 0.5 ohm

92] A 24 ohms and a 8 ohms resistors in parallel gets a combined resistance of...

A] 6 ohms

B] 12 ohms

C] 3 ohms

D] 32 ohms

93] Resistors of the following values are connected in parallel, 5 ohms, 5 kilo-ohms, 50 kilo-ohms, 5 mega ohms] Their equivalent resistance will be very near to...

A] 4.5 ohms

B] 4500 ohms

C] 45000 ohms

D] 4,500,000 ohms

94] The resistance of given wire is 2 ohms] The resistance of the other wire made of the same material having twice the length and twice the cross sectional area is...

A] 5 ohms

B] 6 ohms

C] 2 ohms

D] 8 ohms

95] If the area of a metal wire of a given length is doubles, its resistance will...

A] be doubled

B] be halved

C] remain the same

D] be four times more

96].Among the following only one is regarded as resistance wire

A] gold

B] silver

C] nichrome

D] copper

97] Arc heating occurs when the air between electrodes of opposite polarity becomes..

A] moistened

B] dry

C] ionized

D] none of the above

98] The meter used to measure the temperature of furnace is...

A] hydrometer

B] pyrometer

C] hygrometer

D] tachometer

99] in the case of electrolyte a rise in temperature causes...

A] decrease in resistance

B] increase in resistance

C] no change in resistance

D] none of the above

100] Heat developed in a conductor is proportional to the...

A] square of the power

B] square of the resistance

C] square of the current

D] square of the time

101] Out of the four metal/alloys given below, one has almost no change in resistance for temperature change...

A] nickel

B] nichrome

C] platinum

D] manganin

102] A material that is slightly repelled by a magnet is called ...

A] magnetic

B] paramagnetic

C] diamagnetic

D] ferromagnetic

103] A material that can be magnetized only very slightly is called...

A] magnetic

B] paramagnetic

C] diamagnetic

D] ferromagnetic

104] Substances that can be magnetized easily and make very strong magnets are called...

A] ferromagnetic

B] diamagnetic

C] paramagnetic

D] permanent magnetic

105] A substance that has a high retentivity can be used for the manufacture of...

A] electromagnets

B] permanent magnets

C] temporary magnets

D] paramagnets

106] A substance that has low retentivity can be used for the manufacture of...

A] electromagnets

B] permanent magnets

C] bar magnets

D] paramagnets

107] The symbol for inductance is...

A] H

B] I

C] L

D] X

108] Tube lamp choke is the best example of...

A] open circuited

B] short circuited

C] grounded

D] connected to the neutral line

109] The initial function of a choke in a tube light circuit is to...

A] limit the starting current

B] induce high voltage

C] heat up the filament

D] limit the current after starting

110] The second function of a choke in a tube light circuit is to...

A] limit the starting current

B] induce high voltage

C] heat up the filament

D] limit the current after starting

111] The periodic time of a wave from is 2ms] Calculate the frequency

A] 50 HZ

B] 5 HZ

C] 500HZ

D] 5 KHZ

112] How big is the peak amplitude of a sine-wave with an effective value of 220 volts?

A] 311 V

B] 380 V

C] 400 V

D] 440 V

113] The peak-to-peak voltage is 99V] how big is the effective value of the sine wave?

A] 70 V

B] 44.5V

C] 49.5 V

D] <u>35 V</u>

114] A moving coil voltmeter reads 10 V AC] How big is the effective voltage?

A] higher

B] lower

C] <u>the same</u>

D] 10% higher

115] A moving iron ammeter reads 10 A] how big is the peak current of the oscillation?

A] 7.07 A

B] 1.1414A

C] 70.7 A

D] <u>14.1 A</u>

116] A current of 2 amps flows through a resistance of 10 ohms] The power dissipated in the resistance is equal to...

A] 20 watts

B] 200 watts

C] <u>40 watts</u>

D] 5 watts

117] If the frequency changes from 50 HZ to 100 HZ keeping voltage constant, the inductive reactance of coil connected to supply...

A] remains same

B] become half

C] <u>become doubled</u>

D] become 4 times

118] Capacitance is not affected by...

A] plate area

B] distance between plates

C] dialectic material

D] <u>frequency</u>

119] The capacitive reactance of a capacitor varies...

A] directly with frequency

B] <u>inversely with frequency</u>

C] directly with applied voltage

D] inversely with applied voltage

120] A capacitor acquired 3 coulombs of charge when 6 volts are applied across it] It has a capacitance of ...

A] 0.5 farad

B] 3 farads

C] 3 farads

D] 18 farads

121] A capacitor is connected across a 200 volt AC line, its minimum voltage rating should be...

A] 100 volts

B] 200 Volts

C] 300 volts

D] 400 volts

122] when testing a capacitor with an ohmmeter, the meter indicates some resistance] The capacitor under test is...

A] leaky

B] open

C] good

D] short

123] The total capacitance of a 40 micro farad capacitor connected in series with an 80 micro farad capacitor is...

A] 26.7 micro farad

B] 40 micro farad

C] 60.6 micro farad

D] 120 micro farad

124] For obtaining 1 micro farad capacitor from 3 nos] of 3 micro farad capacitors we have to connect...

A] all in parallel

B] all in series

C] 2 series and one in parallel

D] none of the above

125] In an AC series circuit having R and C the current flowing through the capacitor will be...

A] lagging the voltage

B] leading the voltage

C] in phase with the voltage

D] none of the above

126] If the frequency of the supply is increased in the R-C series circuit the capacitive reactance will be

A] reduced
B] increased
C] having no effect
D] none of the above

127] Power companies are interested in improving the power factor to
A] reduce line current
B] increase motor efficiency
C] increase volt-amperes
D] decrease power

128] A capacitor increases the power factor value of an AC motor load when it is connected...
A] in series with the motor
B] in series with the starter
C] in parallel with the motor
D] in series with the main winding

129] Normally, the power factor of an incandescent lighting circuit is..
A] 0
B] 0.5
C] 0.707
D] 1.0

130] When resistance alone is used to determine current in an RLC series circuit, the circuit is...
A] an inductive circuit
B] a capacitive circuit
C] a combination circuit
D] a resonant circuit

131] Inductive reactance is directly related to..
A] resistance
B] frequency
C] capacitance
D] power

132] Synchronous motor when used for power factor improvement should be...
A] under excited
B] over excited
C] loaded
D] running at no load

133] In a RL parallel circuit, the opposition to total current is called...

A] reactance

B] resistance

C] a vector sum

D] impedance

134] In a AC parallel RL circuit, the power dissipated at the

A] impedance

B] resistance

C] inductance

D] capacitance

135] How much is the nominal output voltage of a carbon zinc cell?

A] 12V

B] 1.5V

C] 2.0V

D] 2.2V

136] Cells are connected in series to..

A] increase the output voltage

B] decreases the output voltage

C] decrease the internal resistance

D] increase the current capacity

54137connected in

A] series

B] parallel

C] series-parallel

D] parallel-series

138] The capacity of a cell is measured in

A] watt-hour

B] watts

C] amperes

D] ampere-hour

139] The primary cell which has the shortest shelf life is

A] carbon – zinc

B] alkaline

C] mercury

D] lithium

140] The cell which has very high energy density for given weight or volume to

A] carbon-zinc

B] alkaline

C] mercury

D] lithium

141] A 100-Ah capacity battery should deliver a current of 8A for approximately...

A] 12 h

B] 8 h

C] 20 h

D] 100 h

142] When the battery is needed to be kept idle for a long time...

A] overcharge the battery

B] remove electrolyte

C] clean the plates with distilled water

D] dry them and store the battery in cool dry clean place

143] The active materials of the nickel iron cell are...

A] nickel hydroxide

B] powdered iron and its oxide

C] 21% solution of caustic potash

D] all the above materials

144] The capacity of a cell is measured in

A] watt hour

B] watts

C] amperes

D] ampere-hour

145] To charge a secondary cell, the system used is

A] low voltage AC

B] high voltage AC

C] AC

D] DC

146] What is the number of phases in a normal industrial supply system?

A] one

B] three

C] four

D] two

147] In a 3 phase star connected alternator, the coils have a phase difference of...

A] 120°

B] 240°

C] 60°

D] 360°

148] Delta connection is used no one of the following

A] primary of the transmission line transformer

B] alternator winding

C] secondary of the distribution transformer

D] primary of the distribution transformer

149] Which method can be used to measure the power in a 3-phase unbalanced load system?

A] one wattmeter method

B] tow wattmeter method

C] three wattmeter method

D] three ammeter method

150] Two wattmeters can be used to measure 3-hase power in a 3-phase, 3 wire system with...

A] balanced load

B] unbalanced load

C] balanced as well as unbalanced load

D] out of balanced load

151] A single wattmeter can be used to measure power in a 3-phase system only when the load is..

A] balanaced

B] unbalanced

C] balanced as well as unbalanced load

D] constant

152] The force producing movement of the pointer in an indicating instrument is called as...

A] deflecting force

B] controlling force

C] damping force

D] distracting force

153] A permanent magnet moving coil instrument will read...

A] only AC quantities

B] only DC quantities

C] both AC and DC quantities

D] pulsating quantities

154] An instrument using gravity control will read correctly if used in..

A] vertical position only

B] horizontal position only

C] inclined position only

D] any position

155] Which one of the following damping methods is used in permanent magnet moving coil instrument?

A] air damping

B] fluid damping

C] spring damping

D] eddy current damping

156] Moving coil instrument works on the effect of...

A] chemical effect

B] heating effect

C] electrostatic effect

D] electromagnetic effect

157] The meter installed at your house to measure electrical energy is an example of...

A] indication type instrument

B] recording type instrument

C] indicating as well as recording type instrument

D] integrating type instrument

158].Which of the following material is preferred for permanent magnet?

A] alnico

B] y-alloy

C] silicon steel

D] wrought iron

159] The instrument which could be classified as absolute instrument is...

A] milli ammeter

B] micro ammeter

C] galvanometer

D] tangent galvanomer

160] Which of the following methods of damping is commonly used in moving iron instrument?

A] Air damping

B] fluid damping

C] eddy current damping

D] viscosity damping

161] The deflecting torque of a moving iron instrument is directly proportional to the..

A] current

B] square of the current

C] square root of the current

D] voltage

162]Which of the following is used for measuring the medium resistance directly?

A] ammeter

B] megger

C] ohmmeter

D] voltmeter

163] An ohmmeter is used for measuring the...

A] insulation resistance

B] resistance

C] current

D] potential difference

164] Which of the following components is not a part of an ohmmeter?

A] fixed resistor

B] variable resistor

C] capacitor

D] battery

165] In shunt ohmmeter, maximum deflection signifies ..

A] maximum resistance

B] minimum resistance

C] a fault in the megger

D] none of these

166].An unknown DC voltage is to be measured, which measuring range will you select first?

A] 500V

B] 50V

C] 1.5 V

D] 0.5V

167].An unknown direct current of micro ampere rating is to be measured, which measuring range will you select first?

A] 20 micro amp

B] 15 micro amp

C] 150 micro amp

D] 500 micro amp

168] A multimeter cannot measure...

A] current

B] potential difference

C] capacitance

D] resistance

169] Dynamometer type meters are used to measure...

A] only AC quantities

B] only DC quantities

C] both AC and DC

D] pulsating AC only

170] Which effect is used in wattmeter?

A] electrodynamic effect

B] thermal effect

C] chemical effect

D] electrostatic effect

171] Which of the instrument listed below operates efficiently as wattmeter in both AC and DC?

A] PMMC instrument

B] dynamometer instrument

C] hot wire instrument

D] MI instrument

172] Electrodynamic type of instrument are used commonly for the measurement of...

A] voltage

B] current

C] resistance D]

173] When the phase and neutral of the energy meter are interchanged, its disc...

A] rotates in reverse direction

B] rotates in correct direction

C] will stop

D] rotates slowly

E] rotates at high speed

174] When the disc of energy meter is rotating even without connecting any load, the error is called

A] creeping error

B] phase error

C] friction error

D] temperature error

175] AC single phase energy meters record the energy in the unit of...

A] kilowatt hours

B] number of thousands of disc rotation

C] volt amperes

D] kilo volt ampere

176] A megger measures resistance in...

A] ohms

B] hundreds of ohms

C] thousands of ohms

D] millions of ohms

177] A megger is exclusively designed for measuring..

A] very high resistance

B] very low resistance

C] ground faults in power lines

D] over loads on DC motors

178] For pipe earthing the minimum internal diameter of galvanized iron of steel pipe required is...

A] 12.5 mm

B] 16mm

C] 3.5 mm

D] 4 m

179] The earth conductor provides a path to ground for..

A] leakage current

B] over current

C] high voltage

D] circuit current

180] if the size of the circuit copper conductor is 10 sq-mm then the size of earth conductor in G.I] wire should be...

A] 1.5 sq.mm

B] 2.5 sq.mm

C] 5 sq.mm

D] 10 sq.mm

181] One calory is equal to,,,

A] 4187 joules

B] 418.7 joules

C] 41.87 joules

D] 4.187 joules

182] The operating temperature range of electrical stove with bare heating element is...

A] 300◦ to 400◦C

B] 500◦ to 600◦C

C] 550◦ to 900◦C

D] 1100◦ to 1300◦C

183] Which appliance works on heating effect of electric current?

A] incandescent lamp

B] bimetallic thermostat

C] H R C fuse

D] toaster

184] What is the size of nichrome wire for heating element of 1000 watts, 230V heater at 500◦C?

A] 18 SWG

B] 20SWG

C] 24 SWG

D] 25 SWG

185] The heat proof insulating material used for heater base is...

A] mica

B] porcelain

C] asbestos

D] glass wool

186].The temperature regulating component of an automatic electric iron is...

A] heating element

B] thermostat

C] sole plate

D] pressure plate

187].The bread toasting zone temperature is about...

A] 400◦C

B] 800◦C

C] 260◦C

D] 975◦C

188] If a winding makes electrical contact with the metal case of the mixer motor the winding is...

A] grounded

B] open circuited
C] short circuited
D] loose connected
189] If the end shafts of a rotor turns blue it is an indication of...
A] scoring
B] overheating
C] freezing
D] burring
190] What type of motor is used in a food mixer?
A] DC shunt motor
B] universal motor
C] capacitor start motor
D] capacitor start and run motor
191] In what position is the motor mounted in most of the mixers?
A] vertical
B] horizontal
C] inclined
D] parallel

Hydraulic System MCQ for Automobile Engineering

1.Hydraulic energy is converted into another form of energy by hydraulic machines. What form of energy is that?
a) Mechanical Energy
b) Electrical Energy
c) Nuclear Energy
d) Elastic Energy
3. Which principle is used in Hydraulic Turbines?
a) Faraday law
b) Newton's second law
c) Charles law
d) Braggs law
4. Buckets and blades used in a turbine are used to:
a) Alter the direction of water
b) Switch off the turbine
c) To regulate the wind speed
d) To regenerate the power
5. ________________is the electric power obtained from the energy of the water.
a) Roto dynamic power

b) Thermal power

c) Nuclear power

d) Hydroelectric power

6. Which energy generated in a turbine is used to run electric power generator linked to the turbine shaft?

a) Mechanical Energy

b) Potential Energy

c) Elastic Energy

d) Kinetic Energy

7. Hydraulic Machines fall under the category :

a) Pulverizers

b) Kinetic machinery

c) Condensers

d) Roto-dynamic machinery

8.Which kind of turbines changes the pressure of the water entered through it?

A) Reaction turbines

b) Impulse turbines

c) Reactive turbines

d) Kinetic turbines

9. Which type of turbine is used to change the velocity of the water through its flow?

a) Kinetic turbines

b) Axial flow turbines

c) Impulse turbines

d) Reaction turbines

10. Which type of turbine is a Francis Turbine?

a) Impulse Turbine

b) Screw Turbine

c) Reaction turbine

d) Turgo turbine

11.How many types of Reaction turbines are there?

a) 5

b) 4

c) 3

d) 9

13.Which kind of turbine is a Fourneyron Turbine?

a) Inward flow turbine

b) Outward flow turbine
c) Mixed flow turbine
d) Radial flow turbine

Pneumatics MCQ for Aeronautical Engineering

1. Fluid power circuits use schematic drawings to:
a) Simplify component function details
b) Make it so only trained persons can understand the functions
c) Make the drawing look impressive
d) Make untrained person to understand
2. A pneumatic symbol is:
a) Different from a hydraulic symbol used for the same function
b) The same as a hydraulic symbol used for the same function
c) Not to be compared to a hydraulic symbol used for the same function
d) None of the mentioned
3. Pneumatic systems usually do not exceed:
a) 1 hp
b) 1 to 2 hp
c) 2 to 3 hp
d) 4 to 5 hp
4. Most hydraulic circuits:
a) Operate from a central hydraulic power unit
b) Use air-over-oil power units
c) Have a dedicated power unit
d) Does not have dedicated power unit
5. Hydraulic and pneumatic circuits:
a) Perform the same way for all functions
b) Perform differently for all functions
c) Perform the same with some exceptions
d) Does not perform all the functions
6. The lubricator in a pneumatic circuit is the:
a) First element in line
b) Second element in line
c) Last element in line
d) Third element in line
8. When comparing first cost of hydraulic systems to pneumatic systems, generally they are:
a) More expensive to purchase
b) Less expensive to purchase

c) Cost is same

d) Cost is not required

9. When comparing operating cost of hydraulic systems to pneumatic systems, generally they are.

a) More expensive to operate

b) Less expensive to operate

c) Cost is same to operate

d) Cost is not required

10. The most common hydraulic fluid is:

a) Mineral oil

b) Synthetic fluid

c) Water

d) Gel

Welding MCQ for Automobile Engineering

40] The angle of below pipe to the line of weld in leftward welding technique is...

A] 40 to 50◦

B] 50 to 60◦

C] 60 to 70◦

D] 70 to 80◦

41] The pressure of acetylene gas for gas cutting a 10mm M.S plate is...

A] 0.15 kgf/cm2

B] 0.5 kgf/cm2

C] 1.0 kgf/cm2

D] 1.5 kgf/cm2

42] What size of the cutting nozzle you will select for cutting 10mm thick mild steel?

A] 0.8 mm

B] 1.2 mm

C] 1.6 mm

D] 2.0 mm

43] The angle of filler rod in case of rightward welding technique is...

A] 10 to 20◦

B] 20 to 30◦

C] 30 to 40◦

D] 40 to 50◦

44] One of the advantages of the high pressure system of gas welding is...

A] it is cheaper

B] it is portable

C] it is less dangerous

D] it does not require a skilled welder

45] Soldering of M.S sheets takes place at a temperature of...

A] 150◦C

B] 250◦C

C] 400◦C

D] 850◦C

46] Forge welding is classified as...

A] fusion welding without pressure

B] fusion welding with pressure

C] non-fusion welding without pressure

D] no-fusion welding with pressure

47] The function of a gas regulator is...

A] get different types of flames

B] mix the gases in the required proportion

C] change the volume of gas flowing to the blow pipe

D] set the working pressure

48] For welding a lap fillet joint in vertical position by gas what should be the angle of below pipe to the line of weld?

A] 30◦ to 40◦

B] 45◦to 50◦

C] 60◦ to 70◦

D] 75◦ to 80◦

49] Name the defect, in which the weld metal is flowing on to the surface of the base metal without fusing it

A] crater

B] overlap

C] lack of fusion

D] excessive convexity

50] What should be the angle of blow pipe between the two sheets while welding a T joint on 3.15mm M.S> sheet by gas welding?

A] 30◦

B] 45◦

C] 60◦

D] 80◦

51] Which metal pipe should NOT be used for passing acetylene gas in order to avoid explosions?

A] galvanized iron

B] stainless steel

C] mild steel

D] cooper

52] he percentage of carbon in acetylene gas is...

A] 99%

B] 92.3%

C] 89.1%

D] 85.3%

53] Acetylene gas contains

A] calcium, carbon and hydrogen

B] calcium and hydrogen

C] calcium, carbon, hydrogen and oxygen

D] carbon and hydrogen

54] In an acetylene purifier the sulphureted and phosphorated hydrogen are removed by...

A] pumice

B] water

C] filter wool

D] purifying chemicals

55].A hydraulic back pressure valve is used to...

A] increase the pressure of oxygen gas

B] increase the pressure of acetylene gas

C] prevent the danger of back fire

D] decrease the pressure of oxygen

56] The nozzle size required to weld a M.S pipe elbow joint with 3WT to get full depth fusion and good penetration is...

A] 5

B] 7

C] 10

D] 13

57] The selection of nozzle for pipe welding depends upon...

A] groove angle

B] welding position

C] pipe wall thickness

D] diameter of pipe

58] One of the functions of flux in gas welding is...

A] dissolve the metal oxides

B] reduce the melting point of mental

C] increase the flame temperature

D] increase the root penetration

59] The angle of vee groove of a single vee but joint for cast iron welding is...

A] 60◦

B] 70◦

C] 80◦

D] 90◦

60] On which of the following factors, the choice of flux for gas welding depend?

A] type of material to be joined

B] type of edge penetration

C] type of fuel gas

D] type of flame used

61].What is the nozzle size required to bronze weld 10mm thick cast iron job?

A] 5

B] 7

C] 10

D] 13

62] State the suitable filler rod for bronze welding of cast iron

A] brass

B] silicon bronze

C] manganese bronze

D] super silicon cast iron

63] In bronze welding of cast iron, the base metal is heated upto a temperature of...

A] 300◦C

B] 650◦C

C] 1000◦C

D] 1300◦C

64] Name the filler rod used for fusion welding of copper

A] manganese bronze rod

B] copper silver alloy rod

C] silicon bronze rod

D] pure copper rod

65] The divergence allowance required for gas welding a 300mm long copper butt joint is...

A] 1 to 2 mm

B] 2 to 3 mm

C] 3 to 4 mm

D] 4 to 5 mm

66] The type of edge preparation done for gas welding a 4mm thick copper butt joint is...

A] single bevel

B] single V

C] double V

D] square

67] The nozzle size used for bronze welding of a 3.15 mm thick copper butt joint is...

A] 5

B] 7

C] 10

D] 13

68] State the filler rod size required for welding a butt joint on 3mm thick brass sheet

A] 1.6 mm

B] 2 mm

C] 2.5 mm

D] 3 mm

69] Name the weld defect which will occur if a No] 3 nozzle is used for welding a 3 mm thick brass sheet

A] undercut

B] burn through

C] porosity

D] lack of penetration

70] The size of nozzle used to gas weld 3.15 mm thick aluminium butt joint is...

A] 13

B] 10

C] 7

D] 5

71] Nozzle size used for welding a 2 mm thick stainless steel sheet as a butt joint is...

A] 2

B] 3

C] 5

D] 7

72] What is the value of preheating temperature for gas welding of aluminium?

A] 100 to 120°C

B] 150 to 180°C

C] 180 to 200°C

D] 210 to 250°C

73] In soldering operation the base metal is...

A] not heated

B] heated to 200°C

C] heated to 650°C

D] heated to red hot condition

74] For welding dissimilar metals, the following property of both the metals should not have wide variations

A] ductility

B] tensile strength

C] thermal expansion

D] wear resistance

75] Name the flux used for brazing of M.S] sheets

A] hydrochloric acid

B] zinc chloride

C] tallow resin

D] borax

76] In progressive gouging to what angle the gouging torch angle is reduced from the starting angle of 30°?

A] 20 to 25°

B] 15 to 20°

C] 10 to 15°

D] 5 to 10°

77] The thermit mixture used in thermit welding can be ignited with an initial temperature of..

A] 1500°C

B] 1200◦C

C] 1000◦C

D] 500◦C

78] Shielded metal arc welding is classified under the process of...

A] electric resistance welding

B] special welding

C] electric arc welding

D] electro gas welding

79] How to specify the size of an electrode holder?

A] by its weight

B] by its shape

C] by its current carrying capacity

D] by the metal used for making it

80] The current set for a 3.15mm medium coated mild steel electrode is...

A] 50 to 80 amp

B] 90 to 120 amp

C] 120 to 150 amp

D] 150 to 170 amp

81] Which method of cleaning you will use to remove oil, grease and paint from the surface of the metals to be welded?

A] filing

B] wire brushing

C] washing with cold water

D] using solvents of diluted hydrochloric acid

82] In the electrode coding ER4211, the third digit of the number 4211 indicates....

A] welding current and voltage condition

B] elongation and impact properties

C] tensile strength of the joint

D] welding position

83] A long arc is used in...

A] welding with a low hydrogen electrode

B] horizontal position

C] plug or slot welding

D] cast iron welding

84] If the travel speed of electrode is high, which type of weld defect you will get on a T fillet joint?

A] overlap

B] slag inclusion

C] excessive reinforcement

D] <u>lack of root penetration</u>

85] Which weld defect occurs on a lap fillet joint due to improper weaving of the electrode in the covering/final run?

A] crack

B] undercut

C] lack of fusion

D] <u>edge of plate melted off</u>

86] A lap fillet weld has uneven bead height] What is the cause for this defect?

A] use of high current

B] <u>low welding travel speed</u>

C] use of wrist movement for the electrode weaving

D] high welding travel speed

87] The coating factor used to make medium coated electrode is...

A] 1.25 to 3

B] <u>1.4 to 1.5</u>

C] 1.6 to 2.2

D] above 2.2

88] Which type of coated electrodes are used for general purpose welding and for training purposes in ITIs?

A] basic coated

B] iron powder

C] cellulosic

D] <u>rutile</u>

89] Maintaining a key hole and use of proper root gap in a single V butt joint will ensure...

A] reducing the arc blow effect

B] faster metal deposition

C] <u>proper root penetration</u>

D] proper reinforcement

90] At what angle the electrode is to be held with the bottom surface of the joint in horizontal position?

A] 60◦ to 70◦

B] <u>70◦ to 80◦</u>

C] 80◦ to 90◦

D] 90◦ to 100◦

91] Upto which temperature a moisture affected (wet) electrode is to be heated for one hour?

A] 50 to 100◦C

B] 110 to 150◦C

C.160 to 200◦C

D] 200 to 250◦C

92] The purpose of presenting the plate while welding a T fillet joint is to...

A] get good root penetration

B] avoid crater defect

C] control distortion

D] control arc blow

93] Lack of penetration in a butt welded joint is due to...

A] too low welding speed

B] short arc length

C] high current

D] low current

94].Which type of distortion can be controlled by presenting of plates to be welded?

A] angular distortion

B] transverse distortion

C] longitudinal distortion

D] distortion due to locked-up stresses

95] What is the percentage carbon present in mild steel?

A] 0.05 to 0.1%

B] 0.15 to 0.3%

C] 0.5 to 0.8%

D] 0.8 to 1.4%

96] If a high carbon steel plate is heated to above its higher critical temperature and then suddenly cooled, it will become...

A] annealed

B] tempered

C] hardened

D] normalized

97] Residual stresses present in a welded job will

A] increase hardness of the weld

B] decrease ductility of the weld

C] crack the joint when load is applied

D] increase the life of a welded joint

98] Which one of the following metal has highest thermal conductivity?

A] zinc

B] copper

C] mild steel

D] aluminium

99] Which one of the following metal has the highest melting temperature?

A] copper

B] tungsten

C] aluminium

D] mild steel

100] Which one of the below given welding machines can be used for both AC and DC welding?

A] engine driven welding generator

B] motor driven welding generator

C] welding transformer

D] welding rectifier

101] The name of the part in a DC welding generator which converts the AC supply voltage into DC welding output voltage is...

A] armature

B] commutator

C] field coils

D] carbon brushes

102] Which one of the following is the reason for poor fusion of bead with the base metal?

A] electrode travel too slow

B] current too high

C] current too low

D] arc too short

103] Which one of the following defects will occurs if the percentage of phosphorus is more in the base metal?

A] slag inclusion

B] surface crack

C] lack of fusion

D] undercut

104] Which method of test you will use to check a surface crack on a mild steel welded joint at a cheaper cost?

A] X-ray test

B] ultrasonic test

C] visual inspection

D] magnetic particle test

105] Which one of the following defects can be tested found by a Nick Break test on T fillet joint?

A] crater cracks

B] surface cracks

C] lack of root penetration

D] insufficient throat thickness

106] Which one of the following metal plates can NOT be joined by projection welding process?

A] tin plates

B] copper plates

C] mild steel plates

D] stainless steel plates

107] In which position of pipe welding, the pipe is fixed and inclined at 45° to both horizontal and vertical plane?

A] 1G

B] 2G

C] 5G

D] 6G

108] The current to be set for welding a pipe butt joint with a 2.5mmØ rutile coated M.S electrode is...

A] 50A to 70A

B] 70A to 80A

C] 80A to 90A

D] 90A to 100A

109] Downhill method of welding of pipe is done while welding

A] a thin walled pipe by rolling

B] a thin walled pipe in fixed position

C] a thick walled pipe by rolling

D] a thick walled pipe in fixed position

110] In which pipe welding position all positional welding is required to be done?

A] 1G (Rolling)

B] 2G

C] 5G

D] 1G (segmental)

111] Which property of cast iron makes it difficult to weld cast iron?

A] high compressive strength

B] hardness and brittleness

C] low melting point

D] low fluidity

112] The type of electrode selected for welding cast iron with mild steel plate is...

A] M.S] electrode

B] bronze electrode

C] low hydrogen electrode

D] stainless steel electrode

113] Name the solution used for cleaning the copper sheets during pickling

A] diluted nitric acid

B] diluted sulphuric acid

C] diluted hydrochloric acid

D] diluted carbon tetra chloride

114] Which type of electrode is used for fusion welding of copper?

A] electrolyte copper

B] copper silicon electrode

C] phosphor bronze electrode

D] deoxidized copper electrode

115] The usual defect which occurs on a weld done by low heat input electrode due to improper cleaning is...

A] undercut

B] porosity

C] overlap

D] crack

116] Columbium based stainless steel electrode is used for welding stainless steel joints] The will prevent...

A] Crack in the joint

B] weld decay

C] distortion

D] spatter

117] Porosity in stainless steel weld is due to the use of...

A] short arc
B] less current
C] damp electrode
D] unstabilised electrode
118] Which one of the following is used in the oxy-arc cutting process?
A] flux coated solid electrode
B] bare wire tubular electrode
C] flux coated tubular electrode
D] bare tungsten arc cutting electrode
119] The electrode holder in a carbon arc cutting equipment is made up of...
A] plain carbon steel
B] galvanized iron
C] aluminium
D] copper
121] for making gutters, roof flashing, hoods etc]
A] Galvanised iron
B] Stainless steel
C] Copper sheet
D] Metal sheets
122] in dairies] food processing, kitchen ware etc]
A] Galvanised iron
B] Stainless steel
C] Copper sheet
D] Metal sheets
123] for making buckets, heating ducts, cabinets etc]
A] Galvanised iron
B] Stainless steel
C] Copper sheet
D] Metal sheets
124] in canneries and chemical plants Metal sheets
A] Galvanised iron
B] Stainless steel
C] Copper sheet
D] Metal sheets
125] Ammonium chloride is used as a flux for soldering...
A] steel
B] aluminium

C] galvanized iron

D] stainless steel

126] Soldering of M.S sheets takes place at a temperature of...

A] 150◦C

B] 250◦C

C] 400◦C

D] 850◦C

127] In soldering operation the base metal is...

A] not heated

B] heated to 200◦C

C] heated to 650◦C

D] heated to red hot condition

128] Rivets for Joining sheets to thick plates]

A] Countersunk head

B] Flat head

C] Pan head

D] Mushroom

129] Rivets for Joining sheet metal]

A] Countersunk head

B] Flat head

C] Pan head

D] Mushroom

130] Rivets for Heavy fabrication work]

A] Countersunk head

B] Flat head

C] Pan head

D] Mushroom

131] Rivets for Reduces the height of rivet head above the meta\ surface

A] Countersunk head

B] Flat head

C] Pan head

D] Mushroom

132] Rivets for commonly used for structural work]

A] Countersunk head

B] Flat head

C] Pan head

D] Snap head

135] Ammonium chloride is used as a flux for soldering...

A] steel

B] aluminium

C] galvanized iron

D] stainless steel

136] Soldering of M.S sheets takes place at a temperature of...

A] 150°C

B] 250°C

C] 400°C

D] 850°C

137] In soldering operation the base metal is...

A] not heated

B] heated to 200°C

C] heated to 650°C

D] heated to red hot condition

138] Soft soldering is done

A] below 450° C

B] above 450°C

C] at 900°C

D] above 1000°C

139] Brazing is done

A] at 1900°C

B] above 450°C

C] at 1000°C

D] below 450°C

140] A brazed joint is

A] weaker than a soldered joint

B] stronger than a solder join

C] stronger than a welded joint

D] weaker than a silver soldered joint

Sheet Metal MCQ for Automobile Engineering

22] Which method of development is used for developing a rectangular tray?

A] triangular method

B] radial line method

C] parallel line method

D] trial and error method

23] What is the profile of the knife cutting edge of the upper blade of the hand level shear?

A] curved

B] straight

C] inclined

D] beveled

24] For what purpose a groover is used in sheet metal work?

A] to make a hem

B] to make grooves

C] to close and lock the seams

D] to strength then the edge of a job

25] Which type of stake is to be selected for making sharp bends, folding of edges of sheet metal?

A] hatchet stake

B] beak iron stake

C] square edge stake

D] tinman's anvil stake

26] Ammonium chloride is used as a flux for soldering...

A] steel

B] aluminium

C] galvanized iron

D] stainless steel

27] Name the tool used to make and finish the leak proof joints of a pipe T joint

A] groover

B] setting hammer

C] creasing hammer

D] round bottom stake

28] Which one of the following metals will not permit X-rays to pass through?

A] stainless steel

B] aluminium

C] lead

D] tin

29] The frequency of up and down vibration of the cutting edge in a nibbling machine is...

A] 1000 to 1500 times

B] 1500 to 2500 times

C] 2800 to 3000 times

D] 3000 to 3500 times

30] Name the instrument used to check the perpendicularity of the branch pipe with the main pipe of a pipe T joint

A] protractor

B] try square

C] spirit level

D] straight edge

31].Which type of notch is used when a single hem meets at right angles?

A] V notch

B] slit notch

C] slant notch

D] square notch

32] To cut out small apertures which punch and die type of machine is used?

A] shear type nibbler

B] punch type nibbler

C] circular cutting machine

D] guillotine shearing machine

33] The overheating of the blow pipe nozzle is to be avoided because it will

A] cause back fire

B] consume more oxygen and acetylene

C] create burn through defect in the joint

D] create undercut defect in the joint

34] State the nozzle size you will select to weld a 3.15mm thick mild steel sheet

A] 3

B.5

C] 7

D] 10

35] The type of flame to be set for welding brass is...

A] air acetylene flame

B] neutral flame

C] oxidizing flame

D] carburizing flame

36] What is the maximum thickness of mild steel sheet recommended for gas welding using leftward technique?

A] 12mm

B] 10mm

C] 8mm

D] 5mm

37].The distance between the root and toe of a fillet weld is called...

A] root gap

B] leg length

C] reinforcement

D] throat thickness

38] Name the weld defect which occurs due to improper cleaning of the mild steel sheet edge and surface

A] lack of root penetration

B] burn through

C] undercut

D] porosity

39] Which of the following mechanical properties of metals gives resistance to pulling forces?

A] toughness

B] ductility

C] hardness

D] tensile strength

Strength of Material for Automobile Engineering

1. What is tensile stress?

a) The ratio of change in length to the original length

b) The ratio of original length to the change in length

c) The ratio of tensile force to the change in length

d) The ratio of change in length to the tensile force applied

2. Find the strain of a brass rod of length 250mm which is subjected to a tensile load of 50kN when the extension of rod is equal to 0.3mm?

a) 0.025

b) 0.0012

c) 0.0046

d) 0.0014

3. Find the elongation of an steel rod of 100mm length when it is subjected to a tensile strain of 0.005?

a) 0.2mm

b) 0.3mm

c) 0.5mm

d) 0.1mm

4. A tensile test was conducted on a mild steel bar. The diameter and the gauge length of bat was 3cm and 20cm respectively. The extension was 0.21mm. What is the value to strain ?

a) 0.0010

b) 0.00105

c) 0.0105

d) 0.005

5. q. Strain is a fundamental behaviour of material.

r. Strain does not have a unit.

a) Both q. and r. are true and r. is the correct explanation of q

b) Both q. and r. ate true but r. is not the correct explanatio of q

c) q. is true but r. is false

d) r. is true but q. is false

6. A tensile test was conducted on a steel bar. The gauge length of the bar was 10cm and the extension was 2mm. What will be the percentage elongation ?

a) 0.002

b) 0.02

c) 0.2

d) 2

7. The lateral strain is ?

a) The ratio of axial deformation to the original length

b) The ratio of deformation in area to the original area

c) The strain at right angles to the direction of applied load

d) The ratio of length of body to the tensile force applied on it

8. The unit of force in S.I. units is ?

a) Kilogram

b) Newton

c) Watt

d) Dyne

9. Which of the following is not the unit of distance?

a) Angstrom

b) Light year

c) Micron

d) Milestone

10. A solid cube is subjected to equal normal forces on all its faces. The volumetric strain will be x-times the linear strain in any of the three axes

when ?

a) X=1

b) X=2

c) X=3

d) X=4

11. A rod 200cm long is subjected to an axial pull due to which it elongates about 2mm. Calculate the amount of strain?

a) 0.001

b) 0.01

c) 0.02

d) 0.002

12. Some structural members subjected to long time sustained loads deform progressively with time especially at elevated temperatures. What is such a phenomenon called?

a) Fatigue

b) Creep

c) Creep relaxation

d) Fracture

13. Find the strain of a brass rod of length 100mm which is subjected to a tensile load of 50kN when the extension of rod is equal to 0.1mm?

a) 0.01

b) 0.001

c) 0.05

d) 0.005

14. In the given figure a stepped column carries loads. What will be the maximum normal stress in the column at B in the larger diameter column if the ratio of P/A here is unity?

a) 1/1.5

b) 1

c) 2/1.5

d) 2

15. The stress which acts in a direction perpendicular to the area is called

a) shear stress

b) Normal stress

c) Thermal stress

d) None of the mentioned

16. Which of these are types of normal stresses?

a) Tensile and compressive stresses

b) Tensile and thermal stresses

c) Shear and bending

d) Compressive and plane stresses

17. In a body loaded under plane stress conditions, what is the number of independent stress components ?

a) 1

b) 2

c) 3

d) 6

18. If a bar of large length when held vertically and subjected to a load at its lower end, its won-weight produces additional stress. The maximum stress will be

a) At the lower cross-section

b) At the built-in upper cross-section

c) At the central cross-section

d) At every point of the bar

19. Which type of stress does in a reinforcement bar is taken by the concrete ?

a) Tensile stress

b) Compressive stress

c) Shear stress

d) Bending stress

20. A material has Poisson's ratio of 0.5. If uniform pressure of 300GPa is applied to that material , What will be the volumetric strain of it?

a) 0.50

b) 0.20

c) 0.25

d) Zero

21. A diagram which shows the variations of the axial load for all sections of the pan of a beam, is called

a) Bending moment diagram

b) Shear force diagram

c) Thrust diagram

d) Stress diagram

22. The stress induced in a body, when subjected to two equal and opposite forces which are acting tangentially across the resisting section resulting the shearing of the body across its section is called

a) Bending stress

b) Compressive stress

c) Shear strain

d) Shear stress

23. What is the formula for shear stress?

a) Shear resistance / shear area

b) Force / unit area

c) Bending strain / area

d) Shear stress / length

24. Which of the following stresses are associated with the tightening of nut on a bolt?

P. Crushing and shear stress in threads

Q. Bending stress due to the bending of bolt

R. Torsional shear stress due to frictional resistance between the nut and the bolt

Select the correct answer using the codes given below

a) P and Q

b) P and R

c) Only P

d) Only R

25. The transverse shear stress acting in a beam of rectangular cross-section, subjected to a transverse shear load, is

a) variable with maximum at the bottom of the beam

b) Variable with maximum at the top of the beam

c) Uniform

d) Variable with maximum on the neutral axis

26. A block 100mm x 100mm base and 10mm height. What will the direct shear stress in the element when a tangential force of 10kN is applied to the upper edge to a displacement 1mm relative to lower face?

a) 1Pa

b) 1MPa

c) 10MPa

d) 100Pa